## Family Study Guide

The Books of Moses Part Two
God Guides His Family and Gives Them His Rules

Genesis 37 - Numbers 14

Firmly Planted: The Books of Moses Part Two
God Guides His Family and Gives Them His Rules

Genesis 37 - Numbers 14

Published by
Real Life Press
P.O. Box 1767
Battle Ground, WA  98604

www.firmlyplantedfamily.com
www.firstclasshomeschool.org
www.thebusyhomeschoolmom.com

ISBN: 978-0-9844323-7-0

Printed in the United States of America

Cover Design by Christi Gifford
www.thegraphiclady.com

Illustrated by
Savannah St. John Bates & Caylin Floyd

# CONTENTS

# A Note from Jay & Heidi St. John, Founders of Firmly Planted and First Class Homeschool Ministries

Welcome to the second book in a series of family Bible study resources that we are calling *"Firmly Planted."*

In Psalm 1:3, David says, "Blessed is the man who trusts in the Lord; he is like a tree, firmly planted by streams of water who yields its fruit in due season and whose leaf does not wither. Whatever he does prospers."

As parents, this is our heart's desire: that our families would be *"Firmly Planted"* in the fertile soil of God's Word, and that as families, we would become students of the Bible. We are told in Timothy that the Bible should be our primary reference tool for life—that "All Scripture is God-breathed and is useful for teaching, rebuking, correcting and training in righteousness, so that the servant of God may be thoroughly equipped for every good work" (2 Timothy 3:16-17 NIV).

While our children are in our care, we have an opportunity to shape their hearts and minds for the Lord. We have an opportunity to teach our children to be amazed by God's creativity as evidenced through His creation. We also have the chance to walk with God in a way that allows our children to grow right along with us.

These books have been designed to help parents with this kind of "growing." We have written *Firmly Planted* with the whole family in mind.

The goal is to get families in the Word together!  As you begin *Firmly Planted*, you will notice that each lesson features activities and questions for every age group. The workbook includes coloring pages for little ones, puzzles that reinforce Biblical truths and more thought provoking questions for older students.

*Firmly Planted* has been designed to assist parents in studying the Bible together with their children. Keep in mind that it's not necessarily the quantity of time you spend in the Bible each day, it's the consistent application of His Word to your life that makes the difference.

Of all the things we have done with our seven children, the time we have spent together in the Bible has proven to yield the best fruit. That's because the real "fruit" we desire to see in our children is never found apart from a growing relationship with Jesus Christ.

Our prayer for you as parents is that you would grow deeper in your walk with the Lord, and in your understanding of His great love for you. Pass it on to your children, talk about it when you rise up, when you lie down and when you walk along the way. Learn all you can about God and His Word.

It's the best thing you'll ever do together as a family.


Jay & Heidi St. John

# Firmly Planted Icons: Family Study Guide

Each component of the Firmly Planted program has it's own symbol. In this way, you can easily see when you finish one section and are starting a new one. The symbols are found throughout the Family Study Guides and the Workbooks.

## The Seed

This is the 'big idea' or 'key concept' for the week. Whenever possible, this will point toward Jesus as He was revealed and foreshadowed from Genesis to Revelation.

## Planting the Seed

*Firmly Planted* offers two memorization options for students. The first, "Planting the Seed," is recommended for ages 4-11.

## Additional Planting the Seed

This is a more challenging Scripture memorization component for older kids. More verses, more challenge!

## Watering the Seedling

Using our 5-6 minute story lesson helps the seed concept 'germinate' for the student. It's also the icon for "Upper Class," *Firmly Planted's Workbook* questions that are geared toward older students.

## Daily Study

As the name suggests, the *Daily Study* is a daily devotion designed to be done with your family. It will guide you into a deeper exploration of what God is teaching in each week's passage.

## Digging Deeper

If you are doing the *Daily Study* with older students or adults, the *Digging Deeper* section is for you. It was designed to be used with the *Daily Study* in order to facilitate deeper discussion and learning within your group or family.

## Taste the Fruit

Finish the *Daily Study* with *Taste the Fruit*, the life-application segment of Firmly Planted. *Taste the Fruit* offers readers an opportunity to apply the life-changing message of the Bible in their own lives.

# Joseph Sold Into Slavery

## Genesis 37

[3]Now Israel loved Joseph more than any other of his sons... [4]But when his brothers saw that their father loved him more than all his brothers, they hated him and could not speak peacefully to him.

[12]Now [Joseph's] brothers went to pasture their father's flock near Shechem. [13]And Israel said to Joseph, "Are not your brothers pasturing the flock at Shechem? Come, I will send you to them... [14]So he sent him from the Valley of Hebron, and he came to Shechem...

[18]They saw him from afar, and before he came near to them they conspired against him to kill him. [19]They said to one another, "Here comes this dreamer. [20]Come now, let us kill him and throw him into one of the pits...." [21]But when Reuben heard it, he rescued him out of their hands, saying, "Let us not take his life..." [22]Shed no blood; throw him into this pit here in the wilderness, but do not lay a hand on him..." [23]So when Joseph came to his brothers, they stripped him of his robe... [24]They took him and threw him into a pit...

[26]Then Judah said to his brothers, "What profit is it if we kill our brother and conceal his blood? [27]Come, let us sell him to the Ishmaelites... [28]Then Midianite traders passed by. And they drew Joseph up and lifted him out of the pit, and sold him to the Ishmaelites for twenty shekels of silver.

They took Joseph to Egypt...

<sup>31</sup>Then they took Joseph's robe and slaughtered a goat and dipped the robe in the blood. <sup>32</sup>And they sent the robe of many colors and brought it to their father and said, "This we have found; please identify whether it is your son's robe or not." <sup>33</sup>And he identified it and said, "It is my son's robe... <sup>34</sup>Then Jacob tore his garments and put sackcloth on his loins and mourned for his son many days... his father wept for him. <sup>36</sup>Meanwhile the Midianites had sold him in Egypt to Potiphar, an officer of Pharaoh, the captain of the guard.

## The Seed

God sometimes uses pain to advance His plan.

## Planting the Seed

And they drew Joseph up and lifted him out of the pit, and sold him to the Ishmaelites for twenty shekels of silver. Genesis 37:28b

## Additional Planting the Seed (Ages 11+)

So Joseph went after his brothers and found them at Dothan. They saw him from afar, and before he came near to them they conspired against him to kill him. Genesis 37:17b-18

## Watering the Seedling

You remember that Jacob, one of the founding fathers of the nation of Israel, had twelve sons. One of the youngest was a lad named Joseph who happened to be Jacob's favorite.

According to the Bible, Joseph was a dreamer who had visions of the future. When he was only 17 years old, Joseph had two dreams where his entire family bowed down before him. Now, because Joseph was his father's favorite and kept sharing his dreams about being a ruler over his brothers, his whole family started to become angry with him.

Perhaps you've been jealous or envious of someone else because that person was more popular or more honored than you were. And maybe you hated that about them, just like Joseph's eleven brothers. It was probably not a very wise thing for Joseph to continue to share his dreams with his family the way he did. Seeds of bitterness began to grow between Joseph and his brothers—even between Joseph and his father. At this point, it looked like the story was going to have a very terrible ending!

Sure enough, things went from bad to worse. One day, when the eleven brothers saw Joseph coming to pay them a visit, they devised a plan to murder him and throw his body down an old, dry, pit so that he would never be found. But Joseph's brother Reuben warned the other ten against killing Joseph, saying "Shed no blood; throw him into this pit here in the wilderness, but do not lay a hand on him." Reuben's plan was to secretly go back later and rescue Joseph and return him to the home of his father Jacob.

But just when it looked like Joseph would be rescued, the other brothers came up with another wicked plan: they decided to pull Joseph out of the pit and sell him to a caravan of slave traders that was passing by. Knowing they would need to cover up their vicious plot, the brothers took Joseph's unique coat made out of many beautiful colors and dipped it in the blood of an animal they had killed.

When Joseph's brothers returned to their father, they

told him a big lie about a wild animal attacking and killing Joseph. Jacob immediately recognized the coat as belonging to his favorite son and he believed the brothers' tale. Can you imagine how hopeless Jacob must have felt? He thought his favorite son had been killed. His house was full of hatred and jealousy. The Bible tells us that Jacob gave up on ever being happy again.

But the Bible also shows us that, even when things look totally hopeless, God still has a plan to make something good happen. The slave traders who bought Joseph from his brothers traveled to Egypt and sold him to a man named Potiphar, who worked for Pharaoh, the King of Egypt. As the story unfolds, we'll see that God is always at work behind the scenes. We will see that God always has a plan for redemption, even when bad things happen.

 **Daily Study**

### DAY 1

Read Genesis 37:3-4

The difficult things we face in life can cause us pain. But God can take our pain and make good come out of it, like he did in the story of Joseph. Jacob made a big mistake in dealing with his children: he showed favoritism to Joseph. This caused a lot of pain in his family. Have you ever known a parent or teacher or coach that played favorites? How did that affect the other people in the family or classroom, or on the team?

 **Digging Deeper**

The Bible warns against playing favorites because it is a very unloving thing to do. In James 2:9, we read that "if you show partiality [favoritism], you are committing sin." Why is favoritism a sin? Why does it cause so much pain? Have you ever felt like someone is being favored over you? Jesus reminds us in the Sermon on the Mount for us to do unto others the things that we would want them to do to us (Matthew 7:12). Or as the Chinese proverb goes, never serve someone a soup you wouldn't eat yourself. Think or share of a time when you have played favorites with other people.

 **Taste the Fruit**

Playing favorites really hurts people. Sometimes we automatically play favorites without even noticing it. Have you ever ignored someone because they weren't very popular or weren't wearing cool clothes? We need to make sure that we treat friends and family members equally and avoid playing favorites. We should never judge people by their skin color, financial status or popularity. But in Joseph's case, God was still at work, ready to take Jacob's favoritism and use it for something good. We will see that later in our study.

## DAY 2

Read Genesis 37:18-21

Anger is a very powerful emotion. When was the last time you were angry? Why were you mad? What did you do with your anger? Joseph's brothers were angry at him and that anger grew into a plan to murder him. Even though God was able to use these violent men and accomplish his plan, their anger still caused a great deal of pain. If we don't learn to deal with our anger, we risk falling into sin. We are capable of doing some very terrible things if we don't manage our anger properly.

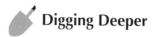 **Digging Deeper**

Anger may be more dangerous than you think! We saw what happened when Joseph's brothers held on to their anger and let it fester and grow. Read Ephesians 4:26-27. Notice that when we fail to deal with our anger properly, we give Satan himself a foothold in our lives! Wow, now that is a great reason to get rid of our anger. What do you think it means to "not let the sun go down on your anger?"

Joseph's brothers certainly should have managed their anger better, but they did not. The good news is that God was able to use their anger to send Joseph to Egypt, where the LORD would use him for His good purposes.

 **Taste the Fruit**

We need to develop the habit of dealing with conflict and anger sooner rather than later. That's what it means to "not let the sun go down on your anger." How does a person do that? First, we need to control our anger and not fly into a rage. Second, we need to talk to the person we are angry with as soon as we can and explain how we feel. Finally, we need to let go of our anger and forgive that person. Are you very good at this process? Which part of this is hardest for you?

## DAY 3

Read Genesis 37:21-24

Most of Joseph's brothers were planning on killing him, but Reuben had compassion on his brother and schemed to save his life. Even though Reuben wasn't able to take Joseph back to his father as he hoped, God still used Reuben's plan to successfully save his life. And the next thing you know, Joseph was on his way to Egypt—just like God intended.

**Digging Deeper**

Seeking to be compassionate can help overcome anger. The Bible tells us to be "quick to hear, slow to speak, and slow to anger" (James 1:19-20). We should be slow to anger because human anger doesn't produce the good life that God wants for us—a life of love and righteousness. It's amazing that Reuben did this because he was the first born son. This means that he would be the one to receive the inheritance and special gifts from his father like the robe that was given to Joseph. Out of all the brothers Reuben had the most right to be upset with the situation. But unlike his brothers, he overcame his emotions of jealousy to realize that it was wrong to kill Joseph.

 **Taste the Fruit**

Do you have a tendency to get angry quickly? How do you feel when you lose your temper? There is one thing we can be sure of: we will always feel better when we control our temper and our tongue and learn to listen. Compassion and understanding always wins out over anger and rage. In Joseph's case, God used the brothers' anger and Reuben's compassion to advance His plan. Only God can do amazing things like this!

## DAY 4

Read Genesis 37:26-28

We should not be surprised when we experience pain; God may just be allowing us to suffer in order to accomplish some greater good. Joseph could have lost faith and given in to hopelessness, But he realized that even being sold into slavery was not the end of the world (Genesis 37:36). In fact, there is no record of Joseph panicking, worrying or fighting for his life. How do you think Joseph might have been feeling? What was he thinking?

 **Digging Deeper**

Psalm 46:1-2 says, "God is our refuge and strength, a very present help in trouble. Therefore we will not fear though the earth gives way, though the mountains be moved into the heart of the sea..." These verses talk about the security that God's people can have knowing their God is with them. The Psalmist goes on to list circumstances that could come up against his city (a symbol for all believers), but no matter what is going on, God brings security. Joseph must have realized this. He must have known that his God would never leave or abandon him. It's through this that he was able to embrace God's sovereign plan later in his life, even when he was in prison! Have you ever felt all alone? Tell about a time when you were very lonely.

 **Taste the Fruit**

Joseph never lost hope. We need to not panic when we are in trouble. Instead, we need to learn how to trust God. What are some things you can do that will help you stay calm and have faith when things aren't going well?

Week 2

# Joseph Saves His Family

## Genesis 42-47

### Joseph's Brothers Go to Egypt

**42** ¹When Jacob learned that there was grain
for sale in Egypt, he said to his sons, "Why do
you look at one another?" ²And he said, "Behold,
I have heard that there is grain for sale in Egypt.
Go down and buy grain for us there, that we may
live and not die." ³So ten of Joseph's brothers
went down to buy grain in Egypt...

⁶Now Joseph was governor over the land. He
was the one who sold to all the people of the
land. And Joseph's brothers came and bowed
themselves before him with their faces to the
ground. ⁷Joseph saw his brothers and recognized
them, but he treated them like strangers and
spoke roughly to them. "Where do you come
from?" he said. They said, "From the land of
Canaan, to buy food." ⁸And Joseph recognized
his brothers, but they did not recognize him...
¹³And they said, "We, your servants, are twelve
brothers, the sons of one man in the land of
Canaan, and behold, the youngest is this day
with our father, and one is no more." ¹⁴But Joseph
said to them, ...You are spies... ¹⁵You shall not
go from this place unless your youngest brother
comes here... they did so...
²⁹When they came to Jacob their father in
the land of Canaan, they told him all that had

happened to them... ³⁸But he said, "My son shall not go down with you..."

### Joseph's Brothers Return to Egypt

**43** ³But Judah said to him, "The man solemnly warned us, saying, 'You shall not see my face unless your brother is with you...' ⁸And Judah said... ⁹If I do not bring him back to you and set him before you, then let me bear the blame forever...

¹⁵They arose and went down to Egypt and stood before Joseph... the men were afraid because they were brought to Joseph's house... ²⁶When Joseph came home, they brought into the house to him the present that they had with them and bowed down to him to the ground. ²⁷And he inquired about their welfare and said, "Is your father well, the old man of whom you spoke? Is he still alive?" ²⁸They said, "Your servant our father is well; he is still alive..."

**44** ¹Then he commanded the steward of his house, "Fill the men's sacks with food, as much as they can carry, and put each man's money in the mouth of his sack, ²and put my cup, the silver cup, in the mouth of the sack of the youngest, with his money for the grain." And he did as Joseph told him...

### Joseph Provides for His Brothers and Family

**45** ¹Then Joseph could not control himself... ²he wept aloud, so that the Egyptians heard it, and the household of Pharaoh heard it. ³And Joseph said to his brothers...

⁴"I am your brother, Joseph, whom you sold into Egypt. ⁵And now do not be distressed or angry with yourselves because you sold me here, for God sent me before you to preserve life. ⁶For the famine has been in the land these two years...

⁷And God sent me before you to preserve for you a remnant on earth, and to keep alive for you many survivors. ⁸So it was not you who sent me here, but God... ¹⁵And he kissed all his brothers and wept upon them. After that his brothers talked with him...

¹⁷And Pharaoh said to Joseph, "Say to your brothers, 'Do this: load your beasts and go back to the land of Canaan, ¹⁸and take your father and your households, and come to me, and I will give you the best of the land of Egypt... ²¹The sons of Israel did so... ²⁶And they told him, "Joseph is still alive, and he is ruler over all the land of Egypt..." ²⁸And Israel said... Joseph my son is still alive. I will go and see him before I die..."

## Joseph Brings His Family to Egypt

**46** ²God spoke to Israel in visions of the night and said, "Jacob, Jacob." And he said, "Here I am." ³Then he said, "I am God, the God of your father. Do not be afraid to go down to Egypt, for there I will make you into a great nation. ⁴I myself will go down with you to Egypt, and I will also bring you up again, and Joseph's hand shall close your eyes."... ²⁹Then Joseph prepared his chariot and went up to meet Israel his father in Goshen. He presented himself to him and fell on his neck and wept on his neck a good while...

## Joseph and the Famine

**47** ⁷Then Joseph brought in Jacob his father and stood him before Pharaoh, and Jacob blessed Pharaoh... ¹¹Then Joseph settled his father and his brothers and gave them a possession in the land of Egypt, in the best of the land...

¹³Now there was no food in all the land, for the famine was very severe... ²⁰So Joseph bought all the land of Egypt for Pharaoh, for

all the Egyptians sold their fields, because the famine was severe on them. The land became Pharaoh's. ²¹As for the people, he made servants of them from one end of Egypt to the other... ²³Then Joseph said to the people, "Behold, I have this day bought you and your land for Pharaoh. Now here is seed for you, and you shall sow the land. ²⁴And at the harvests you shall give a fifth to Pharaoh, and four fifths shall be your own, as seed for the field and as food for yourselves and your households, and as food for your little ones." ²⁵And they said, "You have saved our lives; may it please my Lord, we will be servants to Pharaoh..."

## The Seed

What was intended for evil, God can use for good.

## Planting the Seed

As for you, you meant evil against me, but God meant it for good.
Genesis 50:20a

## Additional Planting the Seed (Ages 11+)

And God sent me before you to preserve for you a remnant on earth, and to keep alive for you many survivors. So it was not you who sent me here, but God. Genesis 45:7-8a

## Watering the Seedling

This week's story is an important one. You might want to snuggle up and pay very close attention. You remember that Joseph was

Jacob's favorite son and that Joseph's brothers had sold him to some slave traders they encountered while on a trip. The slavers eventually sold him to a man named Potiphar who worked for Pharaoh in Egypt. Many amazing things happened to Joseph while he was a slave to Potiphar—some of them bad and some of them good.

But eventually Joseph found favor in Pharaoh's household and he was placed in charge of handling much of Pharaoh's business.

There had been a famine in the land for two years, and the future didn't look any better for growing crops. So Jacob sent ten of his sons to Egypt to see if they could buy grain to feed their families. Jacob's other son by his wife Rachel was named Benjamin. Since Jacob believed that Joseph was dead, he didn't want to risk anything happening to Benjamin so he kept Benjamin at home with him.

The ten brothers went to Egypt and made their request known to Pharoah's manager—who happened to be their brother Joseph. Many years had gone by and the ten brothers didn't recognize Joseph at all. However, Joseph knew immediately that these were his brothers.

Keeping his identity a secret, Joseph tested his brothers by telling them he thought they were spies and not traders. Finally Joseph insisted that the brothers return to their home and bring their youngest brother Benjamin back with them when they returned. This was Joseph's true brother, also born to his mother Rachel. Joseph longed to see his brother.

When they returned with Benjamin, Joseph played several more tricks on his brothers, testing them until they believed he would surely imprison them or make them slaves.

Finally Joseph could stand it no longer and broke down, revealing that he was actually their long lost brother Joseph who was now an important man in Pharaoh's business dealings.

The brothers were very afraid, knowing that they had sold their young 17-year-old brother Joseph into slavery. They thought that God was going to punish them for their sins. They were convinced that Joseph would surely put them all to death or make them slaves for the evil they had done.

Shocking his brothers, Joseph wasn't angry! He didn't hold a grudge—he wasn't the least bit upset. Joseph explained that even though they had sold him into slavery, God had been in charge all along. He tells them God knew there was a famine coming and had placed Joseph in position to help his family and provide food for all of them through Pharoah's riches.

Joseph talked with Pharaoh and they both agreed that Joseph's family, including his elderly father Jacob, should all move to Egypt and live on the best of the land where they would be cared for and fed.

Over the next five years, Pharaoh became more and more powerful, gaining all the cattle and all the land in Egypt because everyone traded their goods to Pharaoh in exchange for food. And during all that time Joseph and his sons prospered because of his favor with Pharoah.

After seventeen years of living in Egypt Joseph's father had grown old and knew he was dying. He asked Joseph to promise to return him to his home for a proper burial and Joseph swore he would obey his father's wishes.

God had promised that He would care for their families and provide for their kin. And that's exactly what God did. He placed Joseph in an important position where he would someday be able to provide food for all of his brothers and their families, as well as his elderly father.

And what's even *more* amazing about this story is that Joseph *understood* what God was doing. Joseph had a choice to make: He could have been angry. He could have wanted revenge on his brothers. He could have been mad at God for allowing all this to happen.

But instead, Joseph knew that God had been faithful all along so he wasn't upset with his brothers when they came to Egypt.

Joseph could have had them all killed or imprisoned or made slaves, but instead he made sure they had all the food they needed to care for their families.

Sometimes we are placed in difficult situations, or we are treated unfairly by someone. But we need to know, just like Joseph, that God always has a plan for those who love God. Even the evil schemes of our enemies usually turn out to be used for our own good.

# Daily Study

## DAY 1

Read or Review Genesis 45:4-18

When someone is mean to you, it's hard not to want to get even, isn't it? God wants us to overcome our desire to take revenge because it isn't our job to punish others; we need to leave revenge and punishment to Him (Hebrews 10:30). Joseph's brothers intended to get rid of him (Genesis 37:20), but he didn't try and take revenge. Rather, God placed him in a position where he could save his brothers' lives later on (Genesis 41:44). In this way the story had a much better ending than if Joseph had just punished his brothers. How do you think the story might have ended if Joseph had taken revenge on them?

 **Digging Deeper**

The Bible says, "Repay no one evil for evil, but give thought to do what is honorable in the sight of all" (Romans 12:17). When Joseph had the chance, he did not punish his brothers. Instead, he reassured them and invited them to come live in Egypt (Genesis 45:9-11). Not only were their lives saved, but they were blessed to live in the very best land of Egypt (Genesis 45:17-18). God is so gracious and forgiving! Joseph's brothers probably deserved to be punished, but the LORD was kind to them instead.

 **Taste the Fruit**

If you've ever been tempted to get even with someone, don't do it! Find a way to encourage or complement those who mistreat you. How could you honor a person who has criticized you? What are some ways you could be nice to them? You will discover that this will help end the conflict much faster than if you had fought back.

## DAY 2

Read Genesis 39:19-20 and Genesis 41:14-15

God proved many times that He could take what was intended for evil and make it work for good. When Potiphar's wife tried to seduce him, Joseph refused to be with her. So she got angry, lied about Joseph, and had him thrown in jail. But while in jail God used Joseph to interpret dreams. He did this so well that eventually he was even asked to interpret the dream of Pharaoh himself. Once again, someone was trying to hurt Joseph, but God used the situation to make something good happen.

 **Digging Deeper**

We already talked about how important it is *not* to take revenge on an enemy. In Luke 6:28, Jesus says, "Bless those who curse you and pray for those

**20**

who abuse you." Sometimes it's hard to pray for someone you don't like! But God tells us to pray about everything in Philippians 4:6, and that includes our most difficult relationships. The very next verse says God will send us peace that will help us get through that tough situation.

 **Taste the Fruit**

How could you pray for an enemy? What kind of things could you ask God to do in their life? If you're not sure how to answer those questions, then pray about that! Ask God to help you learn to pray for those people that are unkind to you.

## DAY 3

We may not know the good that could come out of a situation. Sometimes it will be fairly small, but sometimes the good will be something big! In Joseph's case, the LORD ended up saving the entire nation of Egypt and Joseph's whole family from starvation (Genesis 50:20). Imagine for a moment that your friend lied about you. That would be a bad thing, right? What are some *good* things that might come out of that? Think of one that is small, and one that is big.

 **Digging Deeper**

Read Genesis 49:8-12

Here is one significant thing that came out of Joseph's situation in Egypt. As you know, his family was saved from starvation, including his father and eleven brothers. One of his brothers was named Judah, and it was through his family that many kings of Israel would be born. In Genesis 49, where Jacob makes a prophecy about each of his sons, he mentions this very important fact. He says, "The scepter will not depart from Judah," (verse 10) meaning that kings would come from Judah's family. And of course the greatest king in history would be one of Judah's great-grandchilden—Jesus Christ the Messiah.

 **Taste the Fruit**

What good things will happen when we trust God in tough times? It's often hard to tell. We need to keep our eyes open and watch for the LORD to work in the people and circumstances around us. Then, when we see something good happen, we need to remember to say "thanks" to God. It might be big or it might be small, but every good thing comes from the LORD (James 1:17). Having a thankful heart is always a good thing! Think of something you are grateful for and tell God "thanks" right now.

## DAY 4

Read Genesis 41:1, 14-15

God says He can bring good things out of our bad experiences, but sometimes we may need to wait a long time to see them come about. At one point, Joseph had to stay in prison for two years before the LORD used him to interpret Pharaoh's dream. But finally his patience paid off as he became a ruler in Egypt. Have you ever had to wait a long time for something? Tell about a time when you were waiting for something very important. How did you feel?

 **Digging Deeper**

It takes a lot of faith to just sit still and wait on God. But sometimes we can mess things up if we become upset and worry. Psalm 37:7 says, "Be still before the LORD and wait patiently for Him." We have to remember that God is in control of everything. Bible scholars say that God is *sovereign*. This means, He has a wise and good plan for the world, and He is powerful enough to make sure it happens!

 **Taste the Fruit**

We have to trust the LORD enough to wait for Him to make something good come out of difficult situations. What is something bad that has happened to you? Have you seen anything good come out of it yet? If not, remember Romans 8:28, where it says, "that for those who love God all things work together for good, for those who are called according to his purpose." Hold on to this promise!

# Moses and
# the Burning Bush

## Exodus 1-3

### Pharaoh Oppresses Israel

**1** ⁸Now there arose a new king over Egypt, who did not know Joseph. ⁹And he said to his people, "Behold, the people of Israel are too many and too mighty for us... the Egyptians were in dread of the people of Israel. ¹³So they ruthlessly made the people of Israel work as slaves...

### The Birth of Moses

**2** ¹A Levite woman... ²conceived and bore a son, and when she saw that he was a fine child, she hid him three months. ³When she could hide him no longer, she took for him a basket... She put the child in it and placed it among the reeds by the river bank... ⁵Now the daughter of Pharaoh came down to bathe at the river... She saw the basket among the reeds and sent her servant woman, and she took it. ⁶When she opened it, she saw the child... and said, "This is one of the Hebrews' children..." ¹⁰he became her son. She named him Moses...

### Moses Flees

¹¹One day, when Moses had grown up... he saw an Egyptian beating a Hebrew, one of his people... ¹²seeing no one, he struck down the Egyptian and hid him in the sand... ¹⁵When

Pharaoh heard of it, he sought to kill Moses. But Moses fled from Pharaoh and stayed in the land of Midian. And he sat down by a well...

²³During those many days... the people of Israel groaned because of their slavery and cried out for help. Their cry for rescue from slavery came up to God. ²⁴And God heard their groaning, and God remembered his covenant with Abraham, with Isaac, and with Jacob. ²⁵God saw the people of Israel—and God knew.

**The Burning Bush**

**3** ¹Now Moses was keeping the flock of his father-in-law, Jethro... ²And the angel of the Lᴏʀᴅ appeared to him in a flame of fire out of the midst of a bush. He looked, and behold, the bush was burning, yet it was not consumed... ⁴God called to him out of the bush, "Moses, Moses!" And he said, "Here I am..." ⁶And he said, "I am the God of your father, the God of Abraham, the God of Isaac, and the God of Jacob." And Moses hid his face, for he was afraid to look at God.

⁷Then the Lᴏʀᴅ said, "I have surely seen the affliction of my people who are in Egypt and have heard their cry because of their taskmasters. I know their sufferings... ¹⁰Come, I will send you to Pharaoh that you may bring my people, the children of Israel, out of Egypt." ¹¹But Moses said to God, "Who am I that I should go to Pharaoh and bring the children of Israel out of Egypt?" ¹²He said, "But I will be with you...

¹³Then Moses said to God, "If I come to the people of Israel and say to them, 'The God of your fathers has sent me to you,' and they ask me, 'What is his name?' what shall I say to them?" ¹⁴God said to Moses, "I am who I am." And he said, "Say this to the people of Israel, 'I am has

sent me to you...'" [19]But I know that the king of Egypt (will not let you go unless compelled by a mighty hand. [20]So I will stretch out my hand and strike Egypt with all the wonders that I will do in it; after that he will let you go..."

## The Seed

The great I AM is with His people.

## Planting the Seed

God said to Moses, "I am who I am."
Exodus 3:14a

## Additional Planting the Seed (Ages 11+)

"I have come down to deliver them out of the hand of the Egyptians and to bring them up out of that land to a good and broad land, a land flowing with milk and honey." Exodus 3:8a

## Watering the Seedling

Eventually, Joseph and his brothers grew old while living in Egypt and one by one they died. But the Israelites continued living in Egypt as the years went by and they increased by the thousands.

Meanwhile, Pharaoh had also grown old and died and a new Egyptian king took the throne. He had never known Joseph, and he was afraid of the Hebrews outnumbering the Egyptians. He made them slaves and worked them hard from sun up till sun down every day. Yet the Israelites still increased in number.

Pharoah devised several schemes to kill off the Hebrews' sons to reduce their population, but one enterprising mother hid her infant son and placed him in a floating basket on the river where he was discovered by Pharaoh's own daughter. She loved little baby Moses and adopted him as her own son.

As Moses grew into a man he became increasingly angry at the way the Hebrew men and women were being mistreated and in a fit of anger he killed an abusive Egyptian slavemaster and buried his body in the desert.

Pharaoh found out and tried to kill Moses so he fled Egypt and went to Midian where he met his future wife. There Moses settled happily until one day he was tending sheep when he came upon a bush that was on fire. The bush was burning brightly, and yet it didn't burn up—it just kept burning.

Moses was fascinated of course. Wouldn't you be? He stopped to watch and wondered aloud why the bush wasn't consumed by the fire. Our story says that God told him to stop and remove his shoes because he was standing on holy ground.

You can imagine that Moses was flabbergasted, right? Suddenly, Moses was afraid and he hid his face, too frightened to even look at the bush any longer.

Then God, who was in the midst of the burning bush, spoke again and told Moses that He was the God of his ancestors: Abraham, Isaac and Jacob. God said again in the midst of the burning bush that He had heard the prayers of the Israelites. He had seen the terrible way they were being treated by the Egyptians. God commissioned Moses to go to Pharaoh and demand the release of all the Israelite slaves.

Moses protested, asking two important questions: He wanted to know what God's name was, and why on earth God thought that Pharoah would listen if Moses went and confronted him.

God told Moses that His name was "I AM"—which is interesting, isn't it? Such a peculiar name! It means simply that God always was and always will be. That's all Moses needed to know for now.

The great "I AM" told Moses that He would accompany him to visit Pharaoh. He would perform many miracles which would confirm that He had sent Moses to speak to him.

Finally, God gave Moses specific directions on where He wanted the Israelites to go when they left Egypt. He assured Moses that the land where they were headed was a good and rich land where the people would prosper.

Moses must have left that meeting filled with wonder and many questions. He knew that God had promised to be with him and with the Israelites on the great journey that lay ahead.

God still promises to be with us, doesn't He? Just the way He promised to be with Moses and His people. He is still the great "I AM."

 **Daily Study**

### DAY 1

Read Exodus 3:14

Many people have wished they could be in multiple places at once. It would be very convenient to duplicate yourself to get more done. Although it is hard for us to imagine, God IS everywhere and sees all things.

He saw the Israelites being used as slaves and guided Moses into the house of Pharaoh. He had a plan to save the Israelites but it would take time and patience to see the hand of God deliver them.

Because of this, He can say "I will always be with you" and we can believe it. The one called "I AM" is with His people.

 **Digging Deeper**

In Deuteronomy 31, Moses is giving his final speech to the Israelites and he says in verse 6, "the LORD your God goes with you; he will never leave you nor forsake you." That's exactly what He says here in Exodus 3:14 and Moses carries this truth with him all the way to his death. It's the covenant promise that God made with Abraham and one that continues with His people in our story.

When God asks Moses to redeem His people, Moses says "who am I that I should go to Pharaoh?" Notice that God doesn't just encourage him on his mission, He doesn't say, "you can do it, you're great!" Instead, God assures Moses that He will be with him. This is a theme we see through the whole book of Exodus.

 **Taste the Fruit**

Discuss a little bit what God means when He says "I will never leave you or forsake you..." In Hebrews 13:5-6 the author quotes Deuteronomy 31:6 when he says "So we say with confidence, 'The LORD is my helper; I will not be afraid. What can mere mortals do to me?'." When we live in fear we demonstrate a lack of trust in God's promise. Instead we need to walk in faith when we feel alone, because if we belong to God, then we are never alone.

## DAY 2

Read Exodus 2:11,12

Moses killed an Egyptian who was beating a Hebrew.

The Israelites feared him because of this, and Pharaoh wanted to kill him. He fled from Egypt and wouldn't return for forty years.

It looks obvious to us now, but Moses should have waited on the LORD and not killed the Egyptian. God sees everything. God has a plan for all of us and wants us to listen and wait for His leading.

 ## Digging Deeper

Read Exodus 3:13-14

What's in a name? Moses asks a bold question in verse 13; he asks for God to tell him His name. In asking this he isn't just asking for what God calls himself, but he's inquiring about the very nature of who God is. Names in the Old Testament were often characterizing to the bearer of the name. In the Hebrew language this name, "I AM," is the first person form of the verb for "to be." Later in the story we will see the Israelites call God "Yahweh," He wanted the Hebrews to call Him by this name. "Yahweh" is the same name as "I AM," but it's a different form of the same Hebrew verb. It's as if God's people are calling out "He is." (Note: In many bibles if you see "LORD" in all caps then it refers to Yahweh)

This statement of God is one of ultimate existence. The context that it is placed in means that God is not just saying "I am" in the present sense, but it also has future connotations. So the idea of using this verb is saying that God is not only present with His people now, but He will always be present with them.

 ## Taste the Fruit

Pray to God that He would help you fully embrace who He is as the great I AM. When we pray we get the honor of dwelling in the presence and power of the same God that came to Moses in the bush. The God of Abraham, Isaac, and Jacob. Thank Him for His faithfulness and for never leaving us despite our sin and rebellion.

## DAY 3

Read Exodus 2:23-25

Have you ever wanted something *so* bad but it seemed to take forever to get it? Maybe you're still waiting. The Hebrew people groaned and cried out to God to be delivered from the Egyptians. They were being mistreated and wanted *so* bad to be delivered. Exodus 3:23-24 says God heard their cries and remembered His covenant with their forefathers. God is with His people.

 **Digging Deeper**

The Israelites had to wait a long time in bondage under Egyptian persecution before their redemption. Take a moment to think about another time in Scripture where someone had to wait on a promise of God. In Genesis we saw God make a promise to Abraham that took a long time to come to fruition. God made a covenant with Abraham that he would have a son (but Abraham had to wait almost 25 years!). The Bible reminds us that God isn't "slow" but He's patient with us. Later in Scripture we are also told to wait patiently for the LORD's return. He doesn't tell us when He will come, but we need to trust His perfect timing.

 **Taste the Fruit**

David reminds us in the Psalms, "Be still before the LORD and wait patiently for him" (Psalm 37:7). Sometimes you might have a specific prayer that's not being answered, even if it's a good thing to pray for. A wise man once said, "God's delay is not necessarily God's denial." Think about something that you might be waiting on God for. Be persistent in your prayers and understand that God's delay may not be God's denial.

## DAY 4

If God were to appear to you, what would He look like? If He called out to you, how would you respond? It seems reasonable that the God of the universe would appear as a towering giant with a voice that booms like thunder. That's not how He appeared to Moses. He called out to Moses from a burning bush. That doesn't sound very impressive. But God invited Moses to join Him in delivering the Hebrew people from the Egyptians, the thing they had waited on for so long.

 **Digging Deeper**

Read John 8:48-59

In the book of John chapter 8 Jesus is being tested by the Pharisees and they are talking about the superiority of Abraham over Christ. Then Jesus makes this comment, "Truly, truly, I say to you, before Abraham was, I am" (John 8:58). Those listening picked up stones to try to kill Jesus! Discuss why they would be so mad at Him for saying this...

What Jesus is saying here is profound. It's a claim to deity, He is equating Himself with God, that's why they picked up stones—because it was blasphemy to them. Just like in our story when Yahweh says "I Am who I Am," Jesus says the same thing here in John's account. Before Abraham even existed, Christ was there.

 **Taste the Fruit**

God doesn't just want to be Lord of your Sunday

mornings or your church time, He wants to be Lord of your life. Is there anything that you need to yield to God? He came down in the person of Jesus to die so that He could be with us. The least we can give Him is our life in light of what He's done. If there is an area where you're not submitting to the Lord and what He says, pray about that. Pray that God would lead you in what that looks like, and then do it!

# The Plagues

## Exodus 7-12

### The First Plague: Water Turned to Blood

**7** ¹⁴...The LORD said to Moses, "Pharaoh's heart is hardened; he refuses to let the people go... ¹⁹And the LORD said to Moses, "Say to Aaron, 'Take your staff and stretch out your hand over the waters of Egypt... ²⁰So that they may become blood... He lifted up the staff and struck the water in the Nile, and all the water in the Nile turned into blood...

### The Second Plague: Frogs

**8** ⁵And the LORD said to Moses, "Say to Aaron, 'Stretch out your hand... ⁶So Aaron stretched out his hand over the waters of Egypt, and the frogs came up and covered the land of Egypt...

### The Third Plague: Gnats

¹⁶Then the LORD said to Moses, "Say to Aaron, 'Stretch out your staff and strike the dust of the earth, so that it may become gnats in all the land of Egypt...'" ¹⁹But Pharaoh's heart was hardened, and he would not listen to them, as the LORD had said.

### The Fourth Plague: Flies

²⁰Then the LORD said to Moses, ...say to [Pharaoh], 'Thus says the LORD... ²¹I will send swarms of flies on you and your servants and your people, and into your houses... ²⁴And the LORD did so...

## The Fifth Plague: Egyptian Livestock Die

**9** ¹Then the LORD said to Moses, "Go in to Pharaoh and say to him... ³Behold, the hand of the LORD will fall with a very severe plague upon your livestock... ⁶And the next day the LORD did this thing...

## The Sixth Plague: Boils

¹⁰They took soot from the kiln and stood before Pharaoh. And Moses threw it in the air, and it became boils breaking out in sores on man and beast...

## The Seventh Plague: Hail

¹³Then the LORD said to Moses, "Rise up early in the morning and present yourself before Pharaoh and say to him, ...for this purpose I have raised you up, to show you my power, so that my name may be proclaimed in all the earth... ²³Then Moses stretched out his staff toward heaven, and the LORD sent thunder and hail, and fire ran down to the earth...

## The Eighth Plague: Locusts

**10** ³Moses and Aaron went in to Pharaoh and said to him, "Thus says the LORD, the God of the Hebrews, 'How long will you refuse to humble yourself before me? Let my people go... ¹²Then the LORD said to Moses, "Stretch out your hand over the land of Egypt for the locusts, so that they may come upon the land of Egypt... ²⁰But the LORD hardened Pharaoh's heart, and he did not let the people of Israel go.

## The Ninth Plague: Darkness

²¹Then the LORD said to Moses, "Stretch out your hand toward heaven, that there may be darkness over the land of Egypt, a darkness to be felt..." ²²So Moses stretched out his hand toward heaven, and there was pitch darkness in all the land of

Egypt three days...

**11** ¹The LORD said to Moses, "Yet one plague more I will bring upon Pharaoh and upon Egypt. Afterward he will let you go from here...

### The Passover

**12** ²¹Then Moses called all the elders of Israel and said to them, "Go and select lambs for yourselves according to your clans, and kill the Passover lamb. ²²Take a bunch of hyssop and dip it in the blood that is in the basin, and touch the lintel and the two doorposts with the blood that is in the basin... ²³For the LORD will pass through to strike the Egyptians, and when he sees the blood on the lintel and on the two doorposts, the LORD will pass over the door and will not allow the destroyer to enter your houses to strike you. ²⁴You shall observe this rite as a statute for you and for your sons forever...

### The Tenth Plague: Death of the Firstborn

²⁹At midnight the LORD struck down all the firstborn in the land of Egypt, from the firstborn of Pharaoh who sat on his throne to the firstborn of the captive who was in the dungeon... ³⁰And there was a great cry in Egypt, for there was not a house where someone was not dead...

³³The Egyptians were urgent with the people to send them out of the land in haste... ⁴⁰The time that the people of Israel lived in Egypt was 430 years. ⁴¹At the end of 430 years, on that very day, all the hosts of the LORD went out from the land of Egypt. ⁴²It was a night of watching by the LORD...

 **The Seed**

God uses His power to redeem His people and show He is Lord.

## Planting the Seed

The Egyptians shall know that I am the LORD, when I stretch out my hand against Egypt and bring out the people of Israel from among them. Exodus 7:5

## Additional Planting the Seed (Ages 11+)

The blood shall be a sign for you, on the houses where you are. And when I see the blood, I will pass over you, and no plague will befall you to destroy you, when I strike the land of Egypt. Exodus 12:13

## Watering the Seedling

There were now more than 600,000 Israelite men living in Egypt, plus all of their wives and children. These were the people that God had commanded Moses to organize and lead out of Egypt. Just as He had promised, God went with Moses to confront Pharaoh.

The Great "I AM" gave Moses very specific instructions for each confrontation with Pharaoh, and you can bet that Moses was paying close attention to God's directions!

As you might have guessed, Pharaoh wasn't eager to let more than 600,000 slaves leave Egypt, and besides that we're told that God hardened Pharaoh's heart toward the Israelites. Moses had his work cut out for him.

But when God is working with you no task is too big; no job is too difficult.

God told Moses to announce ten different plagues on the people of Egypt and then God fulfilled each of those announcements just as Moses had said. First, God turned the Nile River into blood. Then He unleashed frogs all over Egypt; then gnats and then flies. Then the Egyptian livestock began dying and the Egyptian people were covered with painful sores all over their bodies. But Pharaoh's heart was still hard and he refused to let the Hebrews go. Then horrible hail storms crushed all the Egyptian crops and then millions of locusts came and ate whatever was left of their crops. As if that wasn't enough, darkness fell over all of Egypt while it remained light where the Israelites lived. By this time you might well imagine that Pharaoh was ready to see Moses and his God leave Egypt once and for all and be rid of all the plagues that had come upon them. But God wasn't finished yet.

God told Moses to prepare for one final, horrible plague upon the Egyptians. He gave Moses very specific instructions on how to proceed and Moses did exactly as he was told.

God said that each family should select a young lamb. The lamb was to be less than a year old and have no sickness or blemish. Then, each family was to kill the lamb and roast the meat for dinner, but they were to set aside the blood of the lamb for a very special purpose.

They were to take the branch of the hyssop bush (which is a kind of mint) and dip it in the blood of the lamb. They were to 'paint' the blood above the front door of every Hebrew house, so that the Angel of Death would pass over them on the night of the tenth plague. God said that He would pass over each of the houses in Egypt during the night and kill the firstborn member of every family *except* for those houses where the blood of the lamb had been applied over the door.

Moses instructed the people in all that God had said, and they obeyed. That night it all came to pass just as God had spoken and there wasn't a single household in all of Egypt where the firstborn didn't die during the night; even Pharaoh's own house. But nobody died or was harmed wherever the blood of the lamb had been painted around the front door. God's people were all safe and sound.

The next morning the Egyptians were wailing and sobbing as you might imagine. Their hearts were broken because so many Egyptians had died during the night. And Pharaoh's heart was broken too. "Then he summoned Moses and Aaron by night and said, 'Up, go out from among my people, both you and the people of Israel; and go, serve the LORD, as you have said. Take your flocks and your herds, as you have said, and be gone, and bless me also!'" Exodus 12:31-32

It had been 430 years since Joseph had brought his people into Egypt during the great famine and now all the Israelites packed up their livestock and belongings. They walked away from Egypt toward the land that God had promised them. Moses and his brother Aaron led them out from among the Egyptians, but not before the Egyptians had weighed them down with gold and silver and jewelry. They were to have the Israelites and their God get out of Egypt and leave them alone to grieve in peace.

And so Moses saw the blood of a young perfect lamb protect God's people from death. Perhaps as you listened to today's story you thought of Jesus, the Lamb of God whose blood still saves God's people from judgment and death even today. Isn't it amazing how God's Word shows us the really important truths in so many different ways?

 ## Daily Study

### DAY 1

Read Exodus 7:1-5

How easily are you impressed? The Egyptian Pharaoh was *really* hard to impress. God did ten supernatural signs that brought calamity on Egypt. These were designed to motivate Pharaoh to release the Israelites. It took ten of these calamities to get him to finally give them their freedom. Pharaoh just wasn't willing to let go of all Egypt's free help. To be fair, God did harden Pharaoh's heart. That is, He made Pharaoh even more stubborn.

God had promised Moses He would free the Hebrews from the Egyptians (Exodus 6:6). To do it, He would show His mighty power so all of Egypt would know He is LORD.

 **Digging Deeper**

Read Exodus 12:21-24

In our story we see the Israelites need to take the blood of a lamb and put it on their doors so the Angel of Death will pass over them. This ends up being a festival that God ordained the Israelites to celebrate, and many still celebrate it to this day. The Passover is very special because its a direct foreshadowing of Jesus Christ. In 1 Corinthians 5 Paul called Christ *our* Passover Lamb, and when Jesus first started His public ministry John the Baptist said "Behold, the Lamb of God, who takes away the sin of the world!" (John 1:29 ESV). We see it in this story and in the gospel of Christ, *only the shedding of blood can save us from death*.

The blood of a lamb saved the people from the death of the firstborn, and the blood of the Lamb (Jesus) saves us from death. But the death that Jesus rescues us from is not just a physical death like in Egypt, but a spiritual death—eternal separation from God. Romans 3 tells us "for all have sinned and fall short of the glory of God, and are justified by his grace as a gift, through the redemption that is in Christ Jesus, whom God put forward as a propitiation by his blood, to be received by faith" (Romans 3:23-25).

 **Taste the Fruit**

Christ is our Passover Lamb, so it is by His sacrifice on the cross that God's wrath will pass over us and we'll be saved from an eternal death. In Romans 3, Paul states that it's by faith that we receive this salvation. God draws us, but we still need to respond by trusting God with our lives. If you haven't entrusted your life to Christ, now is the time. Pray to God and confess your sin, then tell Him that you want Him to lead your life. Tell Him that you understand that it is through Christ that your salvation is accomplished. If you've already put your trust in Jesus, just thank Him. We need to show our gratitude for the sacrifice that He made.

## DAY 2

Read Exodus 7:1

Can you imagine being asked to speak on God's behalf? What an incredible responsibility! Do you think you could do it? Would you question your ability to speak well? To not mess up? To not make a fool of yourself? After all, being the voice of God is a role we never get to perform... Right?

God commissioned Moses to represent Him to Pharaoh. At the same time, God appointed Aaron to be his prophet (a prophet is one who speaks on God's behalf). God was telling Moses what to tell Pharaoh and Moses and Aaron would do it. Pharaoh and the Egyptians must have thought Moses was pretty powerful.

If you are a Christ follower, you have the Spirit of God in you—guiding you, speaking through you, teaching

**42**

you; we *do* have a great responsibility to represent God to the world around us.

## Digging Deeper

Read Exodus 7:2-6

Take some time to discuss the purpose of the plagues. In Exodus 7 God tells Moses, "I will harden Pharaoh's heart, and though I multiply my signs and wonders in the land of Egypt... The Egyptians shall know that I am the LORD, when I stretch out my hand against Egypt and bring out the people of Israel from among them."

God's purposes for the plagues were two fold: He wanted to save His people and make everyone revere Him. In Isaiah the prophet says about Egypt, "the LORD will make himself known to the Egyptians, and the Egyptians will know the LORD... And the LORD will strike Egypt... and they will return to the LORD (Isaiah 19:21-22). God's ultimate purpose for the Egyptians is that they would esteem Him and turn to Him as many did. Quite a few left with the Israelites to follow God and make sacrifices to Him. Even in the plagues God is acting out of love for all people.

## Taste the Fruit

Just like the Egyptians who came with the Israelites, we used to be outsiders. Unless you're Jewish, you are not one of God's chosen people. In Romans 11:17, Paul says we have been "grafted" in to the root, which is Israel. God was not against outsiders, not with the Egyptians nor with anyone else. In the book of Acts the disciples are called to preach to Judea, Samaria, and the ends of the earth! Take a moment to thank God for calling the whole world to a relationship with Him, not just a select group.

## DAY 3

Read Exodus 2:23-25

If God is in heaven, how does He hear us when we call out to Him? It seems impossible to us. After all, we have a hard time hearing those who are nearby, let alone those who are far away. The Israelites called out to God to be saved from the pain the Egyptians were causing them. They must have wondered if God was listening—they had been calling out to Him for years and nothing had changed. But He had heard them and He already had a plan to save them and their salvation was near!

 **Digging Deeper**

Read or review Exodus 8

God was fully sovereign over everything that happened in Egypt. We see the phrase, "as the LORD had said" repeated multiple times throughout these chapters showing us that He prophesied to Moses everything that was to happen. He even chose specific plagues to bring on Pharaoh for two primary purposes. One was pragmatic and the other was to disrupt their idolatry. When Moses turned the water to blood, it poisoned not just the Nile, but the entire Egyptian water supply. This prevented them from drinking and irrigating, both of which were necessary for life. With the second plague, the Egyptians worshiped frogs as well as a variety of other natural creatures. Consequently, God causes them to be overwhelmed with frogs. This not only shows God's power over nature, but it takes the idol worship of the Egyptians and flips it on its head.

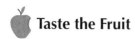 **Taste the Fruit**

Do you have a healthy fear of the LORD? He plagued the Egyptians so that they would revere Him—because they refused to yield to God's power and control. We can have a tendency to see God as our buddy or friend, while forgetting that He is all powerful and deserves a fearful respect. Think about your view of who God is in light of what He is capable of. Let your prayer be that God would bring you into a healthy view of who He is.

## DAY 4

Read Exodus 7:3, 14 and 10:3

What does it mean that Pharaoh's heart was hard? Well, what we see is that when God sends Moses to tell Pharaoh to let his people go, he refuses. He doesn't listen to what God is telling him to do. You might say, "I'm not like Pharaoh, I want to do what God is telling me to do, but how do I listen to him?" God speaks to us in many ways but mainly it is through his Word, the Bible. If you read something that you're supposed to do, don't be like stubborn Pharaoh, just do it!

 **Digging Deeper**

In Exodus 7:3 it says that the LORD will harden Pharaoh's heart. Discuss what this means. Is it fair for God to act this way? We need to understand a few things here in this passage. First of all, Pharaoh's heart was already hard before God chose to intervene. In Exodus 8:32 it states that Pharaoh hardened his heart and wouldn't let the people go—Pharaoh this time, not God. It's important to understand how brutal and rebellious Pharaoh was before the Exodus account. He was prideful and refused to humble himself, then God pushed him over the edge to display His saving power in Egypt.

Romans 9 comments on this account when Paul says, "[17]For the Scripture says to Pharaoh, 'For this very purpose I have raised you up, that I might show my power in you, and that my name might be proclaimed in all the earth.' [18]So then he has mercy on whomever he wills, and he hardens whomever he wills." Isn't this unfair, isn't this unjust of God? Romans 9:14-15 says, "What shall we say then? Is there injustice on God's part? By no means! [15]For he says to Moses, 'I will have mercy on whom I have mercy, and I will have compassion on whom I have compassion.' So then it depends not on human will or exertion, but on God, who has mercy." God never acts unjustly or unfairly. We've all sinned and deserve eternal punishment, but Paul says that all compassion and judgement depends on the God of mercy.

###  Taste the Fruit

You might be grappling with the thought that God chooses who He will have compassion on. Understand that it is not arbitrary. In Romans 9 Paul is careful to emphasize that God is a God of mercy, and His mercy to anyone at all is nothing short of amazing. Take a minute to discuss where in your life God has been merciful to you and then pray and thank Him for it.

# Crossing the Red Sea

## Exodus 13-14

**13** [18]God led the people around by the way of the wilderness toward the Red Sea. And the people of Israel went up out of the land of Egypt equipped for battle... [21]And the LORD went before them by day in a pillar of cloud to lead them along the way, and by night in a pillar of fire to give them light, that they might travel by day and by night...

**14** [1]Then the LORD said to Moses... [3]Pharaoh will say of the people of Israel, 'They are wandering in the land; the wilderness has shut them in.' [4]And I will harden Pharaoh's heart, and he will pursue them, and I will get glory over Pharaoh and all his host, and the Egyptians shall know that I am the LORD." And they did so.

[5]When the king of Egypt was told that the people had fled, the mind of Pharaoh and his servants was changed toward the people, and they said, "What is this we have done, that we have let Israel go from serving us?" [6]So he made ready his chariot and took his army with him...

[10]When Pharaoh drew near, the people of Israel lifted up their eyes, and behold, the Egyptians were marching after them, and they feared

**47**

greatly. And the people of Israel cried out to the LORD... ¹³And Moses said to the people, "Fear not, stand firm, and see the salvation of the LORD, which he will work for you today. For the Egyptians whom you see today, you shall never see again. ¹⁴The LORD will fight for you, and you have only to be silent."

¹⁵The LORD said to Moses, "Why do you cry to me? Tell the people of Israel to go forward. ¹⁶Lift up your staff, and stretch out your hand over the sea and divide it, that the people of Israel may go through the sea on dry ground...

²¹Then Moses stretched out his hand over the sea, and the LORD drove the sea back by a strong east wind all night and made the sea dry land, and the waters were divided... ²³The Egyptians pursued and went in after them into the midst of the sea... ²⁴And in the morning watch the LORD in the pillar of fire and of cloud looked down on the Egyptian forces and threw the Egyptian forces into a panic, ²⁵clogging their chariot wheels so that they drove heavily. And the Egyptians said, "Let us flee from before Israel, for the LORD fights for them against the Egyptians...

²⁷Moses stretched out his hand over the sea, and the sea returned to its normal course when the morning appeared... ²⁸and covered the chariots and the horsemen... not one of them remained...

³⁰Thus the LORD saved Israel that day from the hand of the Egyptians, and Israel saw the Egyptians dead on the seashore. ³¹Israel saw the great power that the LORD used against the Egyptians, so the people feared the LORD, and they believed in the LORD and in his servant Moses.

## The Seed

Nothing is impossible with God the Rescuer.

 ## Planting the Seed

"Fear not, stand firm, and see the salvation of the LORD..."
Exodus 14:13a

## Additional Planting the Seed (Ages 11+)

"The LORD will fight for you, and you have only to be silent." Exodus 14:14

## Watering the Seedling

Moses led the Israelites out of Egypt and God went with them, appearing to them as a pillar of cloud during the day and a pillar of fire at night. God was never out of the people's sight day or night.

God directed Moses and the people to retrace their steps, back to the edge of the Red Sea, and to set up camp.

God moved on Pharaoh's heart once more to harden it and cause him to pursue the Israelites with his chariots and army. God did this in order to prove to Pharaoh once and for all that He was God.

And sure enough, Pharaoh suddenly woke up as if the plagues and the exodus had been a bad dream. He was furious! Just as God had predicted, Pharaoh sent his armies to chase down the Israelites and bring them back once more to serve as slaves in Egypt.

When the Israelites saw the Egyptian army coming after them, they were terrified. They began crying out to

God and arguing with Moses, accusing him of leading them out of Egypt to their deaths. Already the people had forgotten God's miraculous signs. They had lost all confidence in both God and Moses—even though God was in their midst by day and by night. How short their memories were!

Listen to what Moses said to the people: "Fear not, stand firm, and see the salvation of the LORD, which he will work for you today. For the Egyptians whom you see today, you shall never see again. The LORD will fight for you, and you have only to be silent" (Exodus 14:13-14).

And so it came to pass. The Angel of the LORD and the pillar of cloud moved around between the Israelite camp and the Egyptian army. It provided brilliant light for the Hebrews and cast the Egyptian camp into total darkness so they couldn't attack.

Then God told Moses to lift up his staff toward the Red Sea. The LORD would part the waters and make a way for the Israelites to pass through unharmed. Moses lifted his arm and a powerful wind began to blow from the east. It blew all night long and the Red Sea was parted by the wind, which also dried up the sea bed beneath.

The Israelites walked down into the sea between the two huge, towering walls of water on either side. They walked all the way to the other side while their feet remained dry.

Because God had made Pharaoh stubborn, the chariots, soldiers and horses charged down into the water's gap to pursue the Hebrews. But the pillar of fire threw the Egyptian army into confusion as they entered the Red Sea. Their chariots began to crash into one another, turning this way and that. Can you just imagine the deafening roar and clamor of crashing chariots and whinnying horses, shouting soldiers and clanging armor?

In the midst of this, God told Moses to stretch his hand out once more toward the Red Sea and suddenly, the walls of water came crashing down on the Egyptian army. The roaring died away—only silence and the sound of the waves lapping on the shore remained.

The Israelites stood and watched in awe as the bodies of dead soldiers and horses washed up on shore. The Hebrews feared the LORD and served Moses in that awful silence. Not a single Egyptian soldier was left alive. Not a single Israelite was harmed. God, the hero, had rescued His people.

# Daily Study

## DAY 1

Read Exodus 14:15-21

The Bible teaches us that the LORD can do things that are impossible, but sometimes we forget that! We're not used to seeing God do extraordinary things in our ordinary world. God had given evidence that He could do the impossible and proved the people of Israel could trust Him. For one thing, He changed Pharaoh's stubborn heart to let the Hebrews leave Egypt (Exodus 12:31). He also guided them as they left using a pillar of cloud by day and a pillar of fire by night (Exodus 13:21-22). What has God done for you that shows He can do the extraordinary?

###  Digging Deeper

When you think about it, God has done many things to prove He is real and powerful. He created the universe which is so vast, and made one planet that humans can live on (Genesis 1:31). He created your brain, eyes and the rest of your amazing and complex body (Psalm 139:14). He also gave us the Bible, and even though it was written long ago by many different authors, it still changes lives today (Hebrews 4:12). You don't have to look very far before you find incredible, extraordinary things that God has done. These things show us He exists, He is powerful, and He loves us very much.

 **Taste the Fruit**

What are some things God has done for you and your family? Maybe He helped you buy a house or healed a family member of a disease. Remember, the earth, your body, and the Bible are three amazing, extraordinary things the LORD has given us. Make it a point today to notice what God has already done for you. Make a list of some big things and some small things. Then, remember to say "thanks" and tell God that you trust Him.

## DAY 2

Read Exodus 14:10-14

Have you ever been worried or angry about something, and then realized you didn't need to be so upset? The Israelites panicked when they saw the Egyptian army coming after them. They took their eyes off the LORD and their faith wavered. If they had focused their attention on God and remembered He was with them, maybe they would not have worried so much. When was the last time you were really worried? What was going on? How did the situation turn out?

 **Digging Deeper**

There's a story in the New Testament where Jesus was walking on water. Peter, one of Jesus' disciples, asked

**52**

if he could walk on the water too. Jesus told him to go ahead. Amazingly, Peter *did* walk on the water. But when he saw the wind and waves around him, his faith wavered and he began to sink (Matthew 14:28-30). If Peter hadn't taken his eyes off Jesus, would he have been able to continue to walk on the water? Probably. When our eyes are on Jesus, and we remember how great He is, that's when our faith is strong and that's when we are at peace.

 **Taste the Fruit**

We need to keep our eyes on our mighty God when we are facing hard times (Hebrews 12:1-2). The longer we focus on how hard the task is or how strong the enemy is, the more our faith will shrink! The Bible is full of great verses that will encourage us when we are faced with challenges that seem impossible (I Samuel 7:45; Zechariah 4:6; Philippians 4:13). How can you focus on God and His power today? How can you keep His Word in front of your eyes and on your mind?

## DAY 3

When the Israelites came to the Red Sea, with Pharaoh's army right behind them, they needed a miracle! So God divided the waters of the Red Sea and the Israelites crossed over on dry land (Exodus 14:21-22). God did the impossible! He really did! Many people have tried to explain this miracle away. They say the people actually crossed a marshy area, or that the waters were only ankle deep at that time of year. But that doesn't make a lot of sense when you read the rest of the story. No, God can and does the impossible, especially when it comes to rescuing His children. Has God ever done anything impossible or really amazing for you or your family? Have you ever asked Him to?

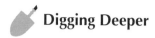 **Digging Deeper**

The Bible teaches us we should not ask God to do miracles simply because we want to be entertained or amazed (Matthew 12:39). We should never treat the LORD as if He is our pet and we want Him to perform tricks for us. We can expect God will do amazing things which will bring Him honor, but we can't expect Him to do *anything* we want Him to do. Why do you think that's true? What are some reasons why God might say "no" when we ask Him to do a miracle?

 **Taste the Fruit**

Sometimes the most amazing miracles from God do not include parting seas or raising the dead. Many times He softens the heart of someone arrogant and selfish, or He draws a person to accept Jesus who said they never would. What are you asking God to do? His Word tells us that at times we don't have things because we don't ask (James 4:2). What are some seemingly impossible things you could pray for? If it's something that God said is important to Him and would bring Him honor, then ask Him again and again!

## DAY 4

Read Exodus 14:26-28

What subject in school is easiest for you? What chores around your house can you do quickly and with little effort? The Bible tells us there is no enemy–not even Satan himself–that God cannot easily defeat. Time and time again God rescues His people when they are in trouble. After Moses and the people crossed the Red Sea, the waters flowed back to their place over the top of the Egyptians. The entire army was destroyed; not one Egyptian soldier survived. God defeated one of the most powerful armed forces in the world, and the Israelites didn't have to lift a finger!

 ## Digging Deeper

The Bible tells us that God is omnipotent. This means He is all-powerful and can do anything He wants; nothing is too hard for Him (Jeremiah 32:17). Some people ask questions like, "Could God make a rock so big He couldn't lift it?" The question is a silly one, but the answer is simple: "Yes, God could make an infinitely large rock, and He could *still* lift it!" The LORD is powerful and can never be defeated by any enemy. That's why we can always look to Him for rescue and help.

 ## Taste the Fruit

It is great to know God can defeat any enemy. We can pray to Him about those who are fighting against us, and He will deal with them. But we need to remember He will do it in His own time and in His own way. Sometimes we want the LORD to step in and squash someone we don't like. But He loves everyone and wants all people to come to know Him and be saved (2 Peter 3:9). What are some other reasons God might wait and wait and wait until He defeats an enemy and rescue His people?

# The Ten Commandments

### Exodus 20

**20** ¹And God spoke all these words, saying,
²"I am the LORD your God, who brought you out of the land of Egypt, out of the house of slavery.

³"You shall have no other gods before me.

⁴"You shall not make for yourself a carved image, or any likeness of anything that is in heaven above, or that is in the earth beneath, or that is in the water under the earth. ⁵You shall not bow down to them or serve them, for I the LORD your God am a jealous God, visiting the iniquity of the fathers on the children to the third and the fourth generation of those who hate me, ⁶but showing steadfast love to thousands of those who love me and keep my commandments.

⁷"You shall not take the name of the LORD your God in vain, for the LORD will not hold him guiltless who takes his name in vain.

⁸"Remember the Sabbath day, to keep it holy. ⁹Six days you shall labor, and do all your work, ¹⁰but the seventh day is a Sabbath to the LORD your God. On it you shall not do any work, you, or your son, or your daughter, your male servant, or your female servant, or your livestock, or the sojourner who is within your gates. ¹¹For in six days the LORD made heaven and earth, the sea, and all that is in them, and rested on the seventh day. Therefore the LORD blessed the Sabbath day and made it holy.

¹²"Honor your father and your mother, that your days may be long in the land that the LORD your God is giving you.

¹³"You shall not murder.

¹⁴"You shall not commit adultery.

¹⁵"You shall not steal.

¹⁶"You shall not bear false witness against your neighbor.

¹⁷"You shall not covet your neighbor's house; you shall not covet your neighbor's wife, or his male servant, or his female servant, or his ox, or his donkey, or anything that is your neighbor's."

¹⁸Now when all the people saw the thunder and the flashes of lightning and the sound of the trumpet and the mountain smoking, the people were afraid and trembled, and they stood far off ¹⁹and said to Moses, "You speak to us, and we will listen; but do not let God speak to us, lest we die." ²⁰Moses said to the people, "Do not fear, for God has come to test you, that the fear of him may be before you, that you may not sin." ²¹The people stood far off, while Moses drew near to the thick darkness where God was.

##  The Seed

Loving God and loving people are the keys to God's demand for obedience.

##  Planting the Seed

Now therefore, if you will indeed obey my voice and keep my covenant, you shall be my treasured possession among all peoples... Exodus 19:5a

# Additional Planting the Seed (Ages 11+)

Moses said to the people, "Do not fear, for God has come to test you, that the fear of him may be before you, that you may not sin."
Exodus 20:20

# Watering the Seedling

It had been about three months since God drowned the Egyptians in the Red Sea. God had been in the midst of His people every day, providing for them food and water.

Then God instructed Moses to have the people clean up and prepare for a holy meeting. He wanted to give them a set of rules that would help keep them in a right relationship with Him. After three days of preparation, God descended from Mount Sinai and made His presence known. He invited Moses to come up the mountain and meet with Him.

God gave Moses ten specific rules for the people to follow if they wanted to serve Him as their Lord.

First, God said they were never to honor any other gods before Him. They were not to worship any statues or carved gods of any kind; not big ones or small ones, not birds or animals or fish.

Next, He said He would never allow cursing or using God's name in vain.

He instructed them to work six days each week but to set aside the seventh day as a Sabbath day–a day for resting.

God told the Israelites they must always honor both their father and their mother. They must also never murder another person.

He warned them against committing adultery and stealing and to never tell lies about their friends or neighbors.

Finally, God told them they must not covet things their friends and neighbors owned. Wishing you had other people's possessions was never allowed!

That was it. God gave ten simple rules for those who wanted to know Him and worship Him.

In God's infinite wisdom, He had give these ten short rules which summed up almost everything the Israelites needed to know about loving God and loving people.

When you're facing difficult decision, look to the Ten Commandments. Ask the LORD to show you what you should do.

Even though the rules are simple, people have always wanted to rebel and do whatever they want, instead of doing things God's way. Perhaps, you've found it hard to obey—you don't do the things you've been told to do. We need to remember that all of God's rules are important—we need to try to obey them.

 **Daily Study**

## DAY 1

Read Exodus 20:1-3

What are some of the rules that you have around your home? Maybe you're not supposed to run in the house or talk with your mouth full. Why did your parents make these rules? Most parents make rules because they care about you and your household. We can be sure that God's rules exist for good reasons! They tell us what the LORD is like: what makes Him happy and what makes Him sad, what He loves and what He dislikes. They also make our relationship with Him and with other people go much smoother. It is wise to obey God's commands and our lives will be much better.

## Digging Deeper

The Ten Commandments tell us how we can live a life that honors the LORD. Jesus said the *entire Law of God* could be summarized in two commands: Love God and love other people (Matthew 22:37-40). Because of this, we know each of the Ten Commandments fit very nicely into one of those categories. And in fact, they do! The first four commands deal with our relationship to God. They tell us to make sure we have no other gods beside the LORD. We are to honor His name, and set aside one day to rest and worship Him. The last six tell us how to relate to each other in honesty, purity and love.

## Taste the Fruit

Which commandments do you think are the most important? Which ones do you think are the hardest to keep? God knows we can never be perfect, but He wants us to do our best to keep all ten. Pray right now and ask God to help you to obey each of the Ten Commandments.

## DAY 2

Read Exodus 20:4-6

What if you decided to obey all the traffic laws except the "stop" sign? Would that be OK with other drivers? Would it be OK with the police? Jesus taught us that all of the commandments are still in force today; all of them apply to us. They give structure to our world and make it safer. In fact, Jesus said not even a single letter of the law should be ignored (Matthew 5:18).

**Digging Deeper**

Have you ever been disrespectful toward your parents? Maybe you have heard your friends talking badly about their parents. It may not seem like a big deal to you, but to God, it is. In the fifth commandment, God literally commands us to honor our parents. It's serious business to disobey and disrespect them. In fact, you cannot honor God without honoring your parents.

Honoring your parents is a foundational part of the Christian life. You see, if you can't honor your parents, you are showing that you love yourself more than you love God.

In Exodus 20:12, we find that honoring your parents is rewarded by long life. If honoring them is low on your list of priorities, make a decision today to treat them with respect and honor. There is a blessing to be found in honoring our parents!

 **Taste the Fruit**

So how do you honor your parents? Like many commandments, it is not always easy—especially when you feel your mom and dad are wrong or if you do not have a good relationship with them. Even though it can sometimes be difficult, it's important for us to remember the fifth commandment when we interact with our parents.

Don't wait for your mom and dad to be perfect. If you do, you'll be waiting a long time! Instead, take advantage of the opportunity God has given you to honor and obey them: for young children, this means simple obedience. For teenagers, it means speaking and acting respectfully toward them, (even when you think you know more than they do); and for young adults, it could mean including your parents in your life in meaningful ways.

If you are a parent, you've probably thought to yourself, "Some day my children will thank me for that!" It's likely that your parents had this same thought about you when you were young. Are your parents still waiting for you to thank and honor them for raising you well? Honoring your parents is a life-long command; it has nothing to do with age.

## DAY 3

Read Exodus 20:7-15

Have you ever broken something made out of glass, like a mirror? Did you just chip the corner a little, or did it shatter in a million pieces? Tell about a time when you broke an object like a drinking glass or a window. God says that if you break even one of His commands, you are guilty as if you had broken every one of them (James 2:10). God has made a way for us to be forgiven, but we need to realize just how sinful we really are. It's like a mirror. No matter if it is chipped a little on the corner or shattered in a million pieces, the mirror is still broken.

 **Digging Deeper**

The Pharisees were the religious big shots of Jesus' day. According to the Pharisees, as long as you had never killed anyone, then you were not guilty of breaking God's command, "You shall not murder" (Exodus 20:13). However, Jesus said if you hate someone and call them a bad name, it is equivalant to murder (Matthew 5:21-22). They are like the mirror that is chipped on the corner—in excellent condition for the most part, but still imperfect and broken. You see, what we think in our minds and what we feel in our hearts is just as important to God as what we do with our hands.

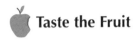 **Taste the Fruit**

We need to realize how sinful we are and how much we need God's forgiveness. Romans 3:23 says, "For all have sinned and fall short of the glory of God." This means none of us will be able to get to heaven just by being good. What have you done to break God's law in the last few days? Did you lose your temper? Tell a lie? Call someone a name? Disobey your parents? Make a short list of three sins that you have committed recently. It's pretty uncomfortable to admit you have sinned, isn't it? It helps us realize just how broken we are, and how much we need Jesus to save us.

## DAY 4

Read Exodus 20:16-21

Tell about a time when you put together a new toy or a piece of furniture. Did you follow the instructions? How did it turn out? If you followed the instructions carefully, and did everything right, the project should have turned out perfectly. Some people look at the Ten Commandments that way. They think that if they follow each command correctly, God will be happy and they will go to heaven when they die. That's not the way it works. The Law of God was not given so that we could keep it perfectly. God knew that would never have happened. It was given so we would realize how desperately we need a Savior.

 **Digging Deeper**

The Ten Commandments are God's perfect standard for all our actions, attitudes and thoughts. Looking at them carefully, we realize we have not kept *any* of them. Have you ever said God's name irreverently? Then you have taken His name in vain (Exodus 20:7).

Have you ever disobeyed your parents? Then you have broken the fourth commandment (Exodus 20:12). Have you ever called someone a hateful name? Then you have committed murder (Mathew 5:21-22). Have you ever wanted to take what someone else had? Then you have coveted (Exodus 20:17). Do you need any more proof you are a sinner in need of a Savior?

 **Taste the Fruit**

We can thank God He didn't stop with just pointing out our sin. He has provided a way for all our sin to be forgiven–past, present and future. The penalty for breaking any of God's commands is death (Romans 6:23). Here is the good news: God sent Jesus to pay the penalty of death so that we can be forgiven and enter heaven when we die. Have you admitted that you are a sinner? Have you asked the LORD to forgive you? Are you trying to obey God and stop patterns of sin? Have you accepted Christ as your Savior? If you haven't, and you'd like to get serious about living for the LORD, then talk to your parents or your pastor. There's no better time than today to ask God to forgive your sin!

# Week 7

# The Tabernacle

## Exodus 25-27

**25** ¹The Lord said to Moses, ²"Speak to the people of Israel, that they take for me a contribution. From every man whose heart moves him you shall receive the contribution for me... ⁸And let them make me a sanctuary, that I may dwell in their midst. ⁹Exactly as I show you concerning the pattern of the tabernacle, and of all its furniture, so you shall make it.

### Ark of the Covenant

¹⁰"They shall make an ark of acacia wood. Two cubits and a half shall be its length, a cubit and a half its breadth, and a cubit and a half its height. ¹¹You shall overlay it with pure gold, inside and outside shall you overlay it, and you shall make on it a molding of gold around it...

¹⁷"You shall make a mercy seat of pure gold... ¹⁸And you shall make two cherubim of gold... on the two ends of the mercy seat... ²²There I will meet with you...

### The Table for Bread

²³"You shall make a table of acacia wood. Two cubits shall be its length, a cubit its breadth, and a cubit and a half its height. ²⁴You shall overlay it with pure gold and make a molding of gold around it...

### The Golden Lampstand

³¹"You shall make a lampstand of pure gold. The

lampstand shall be made of hammered work: its base, its stem, its cups, its calyxes, and its flowers shall be of one piece with it... [40]And see that you make them after the pattern for them, which is being shown you on the mountain.

### The Tabernacle

**26** [6]"Moreover, you shall make the tabernacle with ten curtains of fine twined linen and blue and purple and scarlet yarns... [7]"You shall also make curtains of goats[1] hair for a tent over the tabernacle; eleven curtains shall you make...

[15]"You shall make upright frames for the tabernacle of acacia wood... [31]"And you shall make a veil of blue and purple and scarlet yarns and fine twined linen... And the veil shall separate for you the Holy Place from the Most Holy... [36]"You shall make a screen for the entrance of the tent, of blue and purple and scarlet yarns and fine twined linen, embroidered with needlework...

### The Bronze Altar

**27** [1]"You shall make the altar of acacia wood, five cubits long and five cubits broad. The altar shall be square, and its height shall be three cubits. [2]And you shall make horns for it on its four corners... [8]You shall make it hollow, with boards. As it has been shown you on the mountain, so shall it be made.

### The Court of the Tabernacle

[9]"You shall make the court of the tabernacle... [10]Its twenty pillars and their twenty bases shall be of bronze, but the hooks of the pillars and their fillets shall be of silver...

### Oil for the Lamp

[20]"You shall command the people of Israel that they bring to you pure beaten olive oil for the

light, that a lamp may regularly be set up to burn. [21]In the tent of meeting, outside the veil that is before the testimony, Aaron and his sons shall tend it from evening to morning before the LORD. It shall be a statute forever to be observed throughout their generations by the people of Israel.

## The Seed

God fellowships with us as we worship Him.

## Planting the Seed

And let them make me a sanctuary, that I may dwell in their midst.
Exodus 25:8

## Additional Planting the Seed (Ages 11+)

Exactly as I show you concerning the pattern of the tabernacle, and of all its furniture, so you shall make it. Exodus 25:9

## Watering the Seedling

God began giving Moses some very, very specific instructions on how to build a suitable tabernacle among the people. God tells Moses that He intends to dwell in The Tabernacle and live among the people as they journey toward the Promised Land.

In fact, more than ten chapters of the Bible are devoted to exact details on every aspect of The Tabernacle; measurements, materials, arrangement, design and more.

It is interesting that before God had the Israelites leave Egypt He told Moses this: "When he (Pharaoh) lets you go, he will drive you away completely. Speak now in the hearing of the people, that they ask, every man of his neighbor and every woman of her neighbor, for silver and gold jewelry" (Exodus 11:1b-2).

And that's exactly what happened. "The people of Israel had also done as Moses told them, for they had asked the Egyptians for silver and gold jewelry and for clothing. And the LORD had given the people favor in the sight of the Egyptians, so that they let them have what they asked. Thus they plundered the Egyptians" (Exodus 12:35-36).

So when God began to give Moses the detailed instructions for building The Tabernacle it included the need for a great deal of gold, precious jewels and fabric. These were the exact things God had told the people to plunder from the Egyptians before setting off into the wilderness.

Obviously God was planning on having His tabernacle built even before He began freeing the Israelites from the Egyptian masters. And He wanted the Egyptians to provide the raw materials!

But why? Why would God be so specific, and what did it all mean? Well, several thoughts come to mind.

First, it meant that God didn't want *any* of man's ideas, plans or designs to shape His divine dwelling place. He wanted it built according to *His* plan—not man's plan.

Second, it meant that God cared a great deal about receiving the worship He was due. God had saved His people and set them aside for Himself, and God was adamant that they worshiped Him in the way He desired.

Finally, it meant God was giving Moses the details to make an earthly tabernacle that reflected the true tabernacle in heaven: "They serve a copy and shadow of the heavenly things. For when Moses was about to erect the tent, he was instructed by God, saying, 'See that you make everything according to the pattern that was shown you on the mountain'" (Hebrews 8:5).

The moment Jesus died on the cross the temple veil was torn apart. When He was resurrected, Jesus sat down at God's right hand and became our High Priest.

Paul tells us in 1 Corinthians 10:19, "Do you not know that your body is a temple of the Holy Spirit?" So instead of worshiping in an earthly representation, we now worship in the true tabernacle—our hearts.

Worship mattered to God then, it matters to Him now, and it will matter to Him forever. He promises to be with us whenever we worship Him.

 **Daily Study**

## DAY 1

Read Psalm 19:1-6

Creation was made to worship God. Psalm 19 tells us "the heavens declare the Glory of God," as if the heavens were a mouth speaking the very praises of God. As part of creation, we also proclaim His glory by our very existence. Out of all creation, mankind was the only thing made in the image of God. As a reflection of His image, we have the need and capacity for relationship. Relationship with each other, and with God. God *wants* a relationship with you! This is an amazing thing. The God of the universe cares for each one of us with a unique and powerful love.

 **Digging Deeper**

Unfortunately, the one thing that separates us from enjoying our relationship with God is sin (Isaiah 59:2). To worship God is to surrender everything we are and everything we do. When we choose sin over worship, we separate ourselves from God, and the life of blessing that comes from surrendering ourselves to Him.

He gave His Son so we could have our sins forgiven and our relationship with Him restored. God wants our worship, but we can only give it to Him when we deny ourselves. Jesus says in Matthew 16:24, "If anyone would come after me, let him deny himself and take up his cross and follow me."

 **Taste the Fruit**

What are some important relationships in your life? What do you enjoy about them? What do you do to nurture them? How do you feel when your relationships are not as they should be? Now think about your relationship with God and answer these same questions. Do you relate to God the way you would a close family member or friend?

Take some time to build your relationship with God by talking to Him in prayer. Tell Him you love Him and want a right relationship with Him.

## DAY 2

Read Exodus 25:17-22

Sitting and talking is a common part of building relationships. We have rooms in our houses designed for sitting and talking. Big comfy couches centered around crackling fireplaces and fancy furniture are common sites in living rooms around the world. These are all designed to enhance the experience of building relationships with new and old friends. You may have wonderful memories of spending time with friends and family in places just like these.

God designed the Holy of Holies in the Tabernacle with that imagery in mind. God is holy, therefore, He cannot be near sin. Because man is sinful, the Holy of

Holies was not a place where people could "hang out" with God. Only the High Priest could enter. And only after he was cleansed. But the importance of God's relationship with His people was demonstrated by the beautiful furniture and decorations in the Tabernacle. All of these things centered on the Ark of the Covenant and Atonement Cover or "Mercy Seat." This was where God would meet with the priest to receive an offering of sacrificial animal blood that would allow God to once again fellowship with His people and not see their sin.

 **Digging Deeper**

A cover called the "Mercy Seat" was to be mounted over the golden chest. It was not an actual seat, but rather a chest lid (2 '3 "x 3' 9")—with two cherubim (angels) facing each other on the lid. It was made of a solid piece of pure gold. Apparently, these golden cherubim were to resemble winged angels in God's presence (1 Samuel 4:4; Psalm 80:1; 99:1; Isaiah 37:16). Cherubim were also woven into the curtains that covered The Tabernacle itself (Exodus 26:1-6), as well as the curtain between the Holy Place and the Most Holy Place (26:31-33).

It's important to note that above the atonement cover between the two cherubim is where God would meet with His people. On the Day of Atonement (Leviticus 16:1- 20) the high priest would sprinkle animal blood on the lid. The blood then made atonement (repaired the separation) for Israel's sin (Exodus 30:10). The Atonement Cover was a symbol for Israel of what would be later accomplished by Christ, who, as the Lamb of God, (John 1:29) made atonement for sin (Romans 3:25) by His shed blood (Ephesians 1:7; 1 Peter 1:18-19).

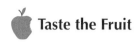 **Taste the Fruit**

The gift of Jesus' sacrifice for our sin is almost too much for us to comprehend. Because of this sacrifice, we can now have a relationship with God.

How did the people before Christ relate to God? The people related to God through the priest. The sacrifice the priest brought into the Holy of Holies was never sufficient enough to cover their sins. It had to be repeated over and over (Hebrews 10:1-18). How has the death and resurrection of Jesus Christ changed the way we deal with our sin? Now, through Jesus, the sacrifice is complete and no longer necessary. Now we relate directly to God through Jesus Christ (Hebrews 4:16). Now His Spirit lives in us, teaching us and guiding us (1 Corinthians 2:12, Romans 8:14). We are new creations (2 Corinthians 5:17)!

Take some time to thank God for sending Jesus to die for our sin. Thank Him for His love for us. Confess anything that might be hindering your relationship with Him. Do you love Him? Tell Him.

## DAY 3

Read Exodus 25:31-40

It has been said, "One of the delights of life is eating with friends." Do you like to eat with your friends? Where is your favorite place to eat with them? God also fellowships with us over food. Here in Exodus 25 we see that God has instructed the Israelites to make a very fancy table to put in front of the Ark of the Covenant. On that table, they were to put 12 loaves of fresh bread each week—one loaf for each Hebrew tribe. The bread was placed there for the priests to eat. This showed God's desire to fellowship with His people. It also demonstrated the spiritual and physical food He provided. The next time you eat bread, remember that God wants to fellowship with you too—even while you eat!

God didn't want the priests to eat in darkness in the Tabernacle, so He provided a way to light the dwelling. We take light for granted in our modern age. In a dark room, we simply flip a switch, and we can see! The Israelites couldn't do that. God had them make a very fancy oil lamp that was always lit. The lamp would light the way for the priests to fellowship with God.

###  Digging Deeper

The lampstand was probably the most ornate piece of furniture in The Tabernacle. It's decorative flowerlike cups, buds and blossoms were formed from one solid piece of gold (31, 36). On each side of an upright shaft were three branches that extended upward (32). Each branch had three flower shaped cups (33), and the center shaft had four such cups (34). At the top of both the center shaft and each of the six branches was a lamp where the flame would burn (37).

The lampstand, which was to burn continually, was serviced by the priests in the morning and at sunset (27:20-21). The amount of gold required for this piece of furniture and its accessories (wick trimmers and trays) weighed about 75 pounds.

Just as the lampstand provided light for the priestly functions before God, so Christ today is the Light of the world (John 8:12). It is He who now reveals the way to God (John 14: 6,9).

###  Taste the Fruit

How does it make you feel to be alone in a dark unfamiliar room? Most people would feel afraid. If it's pitch black, the darkness can feel like it's swallowing you up.

Just like there's a physical darkness that can consume and disorient us, there is also a spiritual darkness that is brought on by sin. However, it is even more consuming and disorienting than physical darkness. Do you know what this spiritual darkness feels like? Can you describe it? There is no light for the darkness of sin except for the light of Jesus Christ. His atonement for our trespasses is the only real and complete salvation we can know.

Take some time to confess any sin that is darkening the light of your soul. Thank Jesus for His sacrifice for your sins, and the light that He brings to overcome it.

## *DAY 4*

Read or review Exodus 26

In Chapter 9 of Hebrews, there is a contrast between the new covenant and the old. In verse 11, the writer of Hebrews says that God created a "more perfect tent" than the one outlined in the first ten verses. The earthly tent is patterned after the heavenly one. God's ultimate dwelling is in the heavenly realms, but He humbled Himself to dwell in The Tabernacle. Even with all the gold and beauty of The Tabernacle, it's not as magnificent as the perfect tent that God created for Himself in heaven.

 **Digging Deeper**

The Tabernacle was important to Israel's national life; it symbolized God's dwelling among the Hebrews (25:8; 29:45), and it was the place where He would meet with the leaders (29:42) and the people (29:43). God's glory was shown in The Tabernacle (40:35). Also, it was the visible center of worship for the newly established theocracy (God-led government). The Tabernacle was a foreshadowing of Christ, who is said to have "tabernacled" (John 1:14), or dwelt, among His people.

The Tabernacle was referred to by other names as well: sanctuary, which means a sacred place (25:8); tent (26:7,11-14,36), because it's built like a tent; Tent of Meeting (27:21), signifying its structure and purpose; Tabernacle of the Testimony (38:21; Acts 7:44); and Tent of the Testimony (Num. 9:15).

 **Taste the Fruit**

When Jesus died on the cross it says in Matthew 27:51 that "the curtain of the temple was torn in two." Why is this significant? It is significant becasue the curtain is what separated the Holy of Holies from all the Israelites except the High Priest. When it was torn in two it meant that anyone could have access to God. This is still true today! We can walk into the Most Holy Place to meet with the Father because His Spirit lives in us. But when Christ died, God's glory and presence (His Spirit) moved from behind the curtain, to the hearts of His people as well. Thank God the Father for sending Christ and thank Jesus for what He accomplished on the cross.

# The Golden Calf

## Exodus 32

**32** ¹When the people saw that Moses delayed to come down from the mountain, the people gathered themselves together to Aaron and said to him, "Up, make us gods who shall go before us... ³So all the people took off the rings of gold that were in their ears and brought them to Aaron. ⁴And he received the gold from their hand and fashioned it with a graving tool and made a golden calf...

⁷And the LORD said to Moses, "Go down, for your people, whom you brought up out of the land of Egypt, have corrupted themselves. ⁸They have turned aside quickly out of the way that I commanded them... ¹⁰Now therefore let me alone, that my wrath may burn hot against them and I may consume them, in order that I may make a great nation of you."

¹¹But Moses implored the LORD his God and said, "O LORD, why does your wrath burn hot against your people, whom you have brought out of the land of Egypt with great power and with a mighty hand?... Turn from your burning anger and relent from this disaster against your people... ¹⁴And the LORD relented from the disaster that he had spoken of bringing on his people.

¹⁵Then Moses turned and went down from the mountain with the two tablets of the testimony in his hand, tablets that were written on both

sides; on the front and on the back they were written. ¹⁶The tablets were the work of God, and the writing was the writing of God, engraved on the tablets... ¹⁹And as soon as he came near the camp and saw the calf and the dancing, Moses' anger burned hot... ²⁰He took the calf that they had made and burned it with fire and ground it to powder and scattered it on the water and made the people of Israel drink it.

²¹And Moses said to Aaron, "What did this people do to you that you have brought such a great sin upon them?" ²²And Aaron said, "Let not the anger of my LORD burn hot. You know the people, that they are set on evil. ²³For they said to me, 'Make us gods who shall go before us... ²⁶then Moses stood in the gate of the camp and said, "Who is on the LORD's side? Come to me." And all the sons of Levi gathered around him. ²⁷And he said to them, "Thus says the LORD God of Israel, 'Put your sword on your side each of you, and go to and fro from gate to gate throughout the camp, and each of you kill his brother and his companion and his neighbor.'" ²⁸And the sons of Levi did according to the word of Moses...

³⁰The next day Moses said to the people, "You have sinned a great sin. And now I will go up to the LORD; perhaps I can make atonement for your sin." ³¹So Moses returned to the LORD and said, "Alas, this people has sinned a great sin. They have made for themselves gods of gold. ³²But now, if you will forgive their sin—but if not, please blot me out of your book that you have written." ³³But the LORD said to Moses, "Whoever has sinned against me, I will blot out of my book... ³⁵Then the LORD sent a plague on the people, because they made the calf, the one that Aaron made.

## The Seed

People are quick to turn away from God.

## Planting the Seed

Then the LORD sent a plague on the people, because they made the calf, the one that Aaron made. Exodus 32:38

## Additional Planting the Seed (Ages 11+)

But the LORD said to Moses, "Whoever has sinned against me, I will blot out of my book." Exodus 32:33

## Watering the Seedling

You remember that God told Moses the ten specific rules He wanted the people to follow; the ten commandments that taught the Israelites how to properly love God and how to properly love other people. When Moses told the people the ten new rules they all shouted loudly, promising they would do exactly as God had commanded.

God then invited Moses to join Him on Mt. Sinai so that He could write the ten commandments Himself on large stone tablets. Moses spent forty days on the mountain with God. During that time God gave Moses the many details of how to build The Tabernacle, the altar, the ark to hold the stone tablets and much more.

The whole time Moses was meeting with God, the people were growing impatient down at the foot of the mountain. Before Moses could come down and give them God's detailed plans, and show them the engraved tablets of God's commandments, the people

**81**

were already disobeying God's orders!

One of the very first rules God gave the people on how to love and worship Him was that they were never to make any statues or images—not animals, birds or fish that might represent God.

And what did the people do? *Exactly* the thing they had just promised they would never do. They went to Aaron and complained bitterly that they had been left alone and there was no god to lead them. So Aaron collected all of their gold jewelry and melted it down and then cast the gold into the shape of a calf. And Aaron said "These are your gods, O Israel, who brought you up out of the land of Egypt!" Can you believe it?

In less than a month the people had already broken the first two commandments. When they saw the golden calf that Aaron had made they began to dance and sing and worship the metal statue. In fact, they threw the wildest party you can possibly imagine.

Even though the people had forgotten about God, He knew what they were doing. God told Moses He was going to destroy the Israelites because of the awful thing they had done. But Moses pleaded for them, telling God that if He killed the Israelites, the Egyptians would have the last laugh and say that God only brought His people out of Egypt so He could kill them. So God listened to Moses' plea.

When Moses came back down from the mountain, he was appalled at the party he saw going on. He was so angry he threw down the stone tablets that God had written on, breaking them. Moses demanded an explanation from Aaron who had little to say, so Moses destroyed the golden calf. The sons of Levi rallied around Moses and killed many who had sinned against God.

Sad and exhausted, Moses climbed the mountain once more and tried to strike a bargain with God to make up for the sins of the people. God told Moses to continue on his journey toward the Promised Land, but God sent a plague to punish the people who had thrown the wild party and worshipped the false idol.

God's plans were very specific, but once again people rebelled and wanted to do things their own way. But remember—God was working on a plan for redemption and rescue through His Son Jesus—the Savior, the Messiah.

## Daily Study

### DAY 1

Read Exodus 24:1-4

Can you remember a time when your parents asked you to do your chores but you didn't end up doing them? Maybe you heard your parents clearly; maybe you had even thought, "I really should do my chores." But in the end you didn't do them. What are some reasons why you may not have actually done your chores?

Hearing God's commands is important, but real obedience is actually *doing* what God has commanded. The people had heard the Ten Commandments and said they would obey (Exodus 24:3). But it took less than 40 days for the people to change their minds and start worshiping an idol.

 **Digging Deeper**

James 1:22-25 tells us why it is important that we don't just *hear* God's commands, but that we *do* them as well. If we say we love God but we don't do what He commands, then we are probably not very serious about being a Christian. We might think our lives are

pleasing to the LORD, but we are really just fooling ourselves (verse 22). Jesus said it this way in John 14:21, "Whoever has my commandments and keeps them, ...loves me."

James also says that God will bless those who hear His commands and obeys them (verse 25). When we disobey God, we sin. And sin always messes things up or brings pain. When we don't love others we get into a lot of arguments and fights. When we don't obey our parents, we end up getting disciplined. If we obey God, our lives will go much, much smoother! God gives peace and joy to those who are careful to obey Him (Deuteronomy 30:16).

 ## Taste the Fruit

Sometimes we are quick to criticize the people of Israel for turning away from God and worshiping an idol. But isn't it true that we are quick to disobey God, too? Even when we know He has told us to obey our parents, we still disobey. We know we shouldn't lie, but we still exaggerate and stretch the truth. We can be a lot like the disobedient Hebrews, can't we?

If we say we love God, then we should show it by being quick to obey Him. We need to actively obey the LORD by doing what He has commanded. Read the Bible, listen to what God tells you to do ... then go out and do it! Be kind to your brothers and sisters. Do your chores without being told. Do your best in school and don't be lazy. There are many, many ways for all of us to get serious about obeying God and doing what He commands!

Take some time right now to pray that God would help you to do what He tells you to do. Ask the LORD to give you the strength to follow His commands.

# DAY 2

Read Exodus 32:21-24

Tell about a time when you got blamed for something someone else did. Or maybe *you* tried to blame someone else for some wrong thing you did. It's almost automatic; our first tendency is to try and blame others for our sin. Maybe it's because we're embarrassed, or we want to hide our mistakes, or we really don't think we are at fault. No matter the reason, we usually try and escape responsibility for our sin and errors.

In the story of the golden calf, Aaron tried to pass blame for what he had done. In Exodus 32:21-24, Moses confronted him about making the idol. But instead of admitting his own sin, Aaron talked only about how evil the people were. Next, he pointed to the fact that the people told him to make the idol. Then, in the lamest excuse of all, he said he just threw a bunch of gold jewelry in the fire and out popped a golden calf! This is a classic example of trying to blame others for our sins.

 **Digging Deeper**

The Bible teaches very clearly that we are all sinners. Romans 3:23 tells us that "all have sinned." This means every person that has ever lived. No one is perfect because we have all done wrong things. It doesn't matter how big or small the sin. If we have told even one lie or been unkind to someone only once, we are guilty of sin.

Furthermore, because we are all sinners, the Bible tells us that we can't blame our sin on other people. We are guilty and we deserve to be punished for the sins that we have committed. The good news is that Jesus died on the cross: He took the punishment that we deserved. Jesus had to die because *we were guilty*. Ezekiel 18:4 tells us that "the soul who sins shall die." Jesus died in our place because there is a penalty for sin.

 **Taste the Fruit**

God doesn't expect us to be perfect. He just wants us to admit when we are wrong and take responsibility for our mistakes. If we never admit we have a problem with sin, how are we ever going to overcome it?

Don't be like Aaron and make a bunch of lame excuses when you do something wrong. If you hurt someone, go to them and say you are sorry and that you will try not to hurt them again. Then go to God and ask for His forgiveness. Remember that we hurt people *and* God when we sin and we need to apologize to them both when we do wrong things.

Pray right now and ask God to help you be willing to say, "I'm sorry." It may seem very hard—and it is sometimes! But you will always be happier and more at peace if you will accept responsibility for your sin.

## DAY 3

Read Exodus 32:30-35

Do you have a hard time making up your mind? When was the last time you struggled to make a decision? Tell the story of a time when you couldn't decide what movie to watch or what kind of ice cream you wanted for dessert.

In the story of the golden calf, the LORD was very angry at Aaron and the people of Israel for creating and worshiping an idol. He was so angry, in fact, that He told Moses He was going to wipe out the entire nation! It seemed like this was the end for the Hebrews. But just before God wiped Israel out, He changed His mind and did not destroy them. What do you think about this? Does it sound like God couldn't make up His mind?

The important thing to remember is that God loves to extend grace to sinners. He often relents from sending judgment even when it's deserved. Since the LORD is the creator of the universe, He certainly has the right to judge... and to change His mind. We can be sure He will never ignore sin or pretend it didn't happen. But we can be just as sure that God loves to show compassion, even to the most undeserving person (Romans 5:8).

 **Digging Deeper**

Even if you don't know much about the Bible, you've probably heard the story of Jonah. Most people focus on the part where Jonah is thrown into the sea and swallowed by a great fish! That part is all very interesting, but that's not the main point of the story. The central theme of the book of Jonah is the great compassion of the Lord. God said He was going to destroy the evil city of Nineveh, but when the people humbled themselves and were sorry for their sin, the Bible says God "relented" and didn't judge them like He said He would.

Here's something really interesting about this story: Jonah was actually angry at God for sparing the people of Nineveh! This shows how easy it is for us to lack compassion for others and demonstrates the incredible compassion of God. Even when we think that people deserve to be punished for their sin, God steps in and is willing to forgive. His grace is amazing, isn't it?

Romans 6:23 is a well known Bible verse. It contains both the bad news that we are sinners deserving punishment, and the good news that God wants to forgive us. It says, "For the wages of sin is death, but the free gift of God is eternal life in Christ Jesus our Lord."

**87**

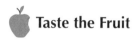 **Taste the Fruit**

We need to appreciate the great compassion of the LORD. Like Jonah, it is easy for us to want to see sinners punished. But when we stop to consider how much we ourselves have been forgiven, then it will be a little easier to extend grace to others.

How can you show compassion to others today? Even when you think someone deserves to be punished, be kind to them instead. Offer forgiveness instead of judgment. Give a compliment instead of criticism. Pray right now that God will give you a heart that is tender and compassionate toward others.

## *DAY 4*

Read Exodus 32:20

Do you know what the word "repentance" means? It means to be really sorry for the wrong things you have done, and then to do your best to never do them again. In the story of the golden calf, it appears that the people never truly repented of their sin. Because of this, they were punished a number of times for worshiping an idol (Exodus 32:20, 27-28, 35).

Have you ever had a hard a time saying you were sorry? If you don't think so, see how it feels the next time you have to admit to your parents or one of your brothers or sisters that you were wrong! It is very important that we are able to humble ourselves. Otherwise God, our parents or someone else will have to do it. Then the consequences could be much more painful.

 **Digging Deeper**

One of the most amazing things about God is that He is omniscient, meaning that He knows everything (Psalm 147:4-5). He always instantly knows the right answer to every question; He never has to stop and figure something out. He always knows exactly what to do, even in the toughest situations.

God's omniscience also means that He knows even the deepest thoughts and secrets of our hearts. We can never fool Him or get away with any sin, no matter how big or small. The LORD is always, always ready to forgive us if we will humbly admit that we are wrong. But if we don't repent, we can be sure that our sins will catch up with us. God loves us too much to let us get away with sins that will mess up our lives. Hebrews 12:5-6 tells us that God disciplines us like any loving father would discipline His children.

 **Taste the Fruit**

We all need to say we are sorry when we hurt someone or do something wrong. And if we are *truly* sorry about our sin, we will try very hard to not do them again. What are some of the sins that you struggle with? Look for a chance today to apologize for something you have done wrong and then ask God to help you not to that thing again. Don't follow the example of the people of Israel! Don't be stubborn, "stiff-necked" and refuse to admit when you are wrong.

If you really want to learn to humble yourself and repent, you will have lots of chances to do so in the days ahead. Why don't you stop and pray right now? Ask God to remind you when you need to say you're sorry for your sin. Then ask Him for the strength to not commit that sin again.

# Choosing the Levites

## Numbers 3

**3** ²Nadab the firstborn, and Abihu, Eleazar, and Ithamar. ³These are the names of the sons of Aaron, the anointed priests...

**Duties of the Levites**

⁵And the Lᴏʀᴅ spoke to Moses, saying, ⁶"Bring the tribe of Levi near, and set them before Aaron the priest, that they may minister to him. ⁷They shall keep guard over him and over the whole congregation before the tent of meeting, as they minister at the tabernacle. ⁸They shall guard all the furnishings of the tent of meeting, and keep guard over the people of Israel as they minister at the tabernacle... ¹⁰And you shall appoint Aaron and his sons, and they shall guard their priesthood. But if any outsider comes near, he shall be put to death."

¹¹And the Lᴏʀᴅ spoke to Moses, saying, ¹²"Behold, I have taken the Levites from among the people of Israel instead of every firstborn who opens the womb among the people of Israel. The Levites shall be mine, ¹³for all the firstborn are mine. On the day that I struck down all the firstborn in the land of Egypt, I consecrated for my own all the firstborn in Israel, both of man and of beast. They shall be mine: I am the Lᴏʀᴅ..."

There were 8,600, keeping guard over the sanctuary... ³²And Eleazar the son of Aaron the priest was to be chief over the chiefs of the Levites, and to have oversight of those who kept guard over the sanctuary...

[38]Those who were to camp before the tabernacle on the east, before the tent of meeting toward the sunrise, were Moses and Aaron and his sons, guarding the sanctuary itself, to protect the people of Israel. And any outsider who came near was to be put to death. [39]All those listed among the Levites, whom Moses and Aaron listed at the commandment of the Lord, by clans, all the males from a month old and upward, were 22,000.

## Redemption of the Firstborn

[40]And the Lord said to Moses, "List all the firstborn males of the people of Israel, from a month old and upward..." [43]And all the firstborn males, according to the number of names, from a month old and upward as listed were 22,273.

[44]And the Lord spoke to Moses, saying, [45]"Take the Levites instead of all the firstborn among the people of Israel, and the cattle of the Levites instead of their cattle. The Levites shall be mine: I am the Lord. [46]And as the redemption price for the 273 of the firstborn of the people of Israel, over and above the number of the male Levites, [47]you shall take five shekels per head; you shall take them according to the shekel of the sanctuary (the shekel of twenty gerahs), [48]and give the money to Aaron and his sons as the redemption price for those who are over..." [50]He took the money, 1,365 shekels, by the shekel of the sanctuary. [51]And Moses gave the redemption money to Aaron and his sons, according to the word of the Lord, as the Lord commanded Moses.

## The Seed

Priests are special servants of God.

 ## Planting the Seed

And the LORD spoke to Moses, saying, "Behold, I have taken the Levites from among the people of Israel... The Levites shall be mine..." Numbers 3:11,12b

## Additional Planting the Seed (Ages 11+)

But when Christ appeared as a high priest... he entered once for all into the holy places, not by means of the blood of goats and calves but by means of his own blood... Hebrews 9:11a,12

 ## Watering the Seedling

God gave very specific instructions for how He wanted The Tabernacle and all its furnishings to be built. They were the earthly representation of the real tabernacle in heaven. Next, He began to give detailed directions on how the priests who serve in the temple were to be chosen.

God directed Moses and Aaron to select 22,000 Levites to serve as priests and guards in the temple. He then gave specific directions on how and where each of the Levites were to perform their duty. God even made provision for the feeding and care of the newly appointed priesthood.

Clearly, the LORD felt these men were valuable! The Levites were doing an important job among the people of Israel. In fact, He numbered them down to the very last man.

The Levites performed the vital task of making sacrifices. The high priest went once each year into the Holy of Holies to atone for the sins of God's people. This was done by sprinkling the blood of sacrificed animals on the altar.

Listen to the words of the author of Hebrews in Chapter 9 beginning in verse 23: "Thus it was necessary for the copies of the heavenly things to be purified with these rites, but the heavenly things themselves with better sacrifices than these. For Christ has entered, not into holy places made with hands, which are copies of the true things, but into heaven itself, now to appear in the presence of God on our behalf. Nor was it to offer himself repeatedly, as the high priest enters the holy places every year with blood not his own, for then he would have had to suffer repeatedly since the foundation of the world. But as it is, he has appeared once for all at the end of the ages to put away sin by the sacrifice of himself. And just as it is appointed for man to die once, and after that comes judgment, so Christ, having been offered once to bear the sins of many, will appear a second time, not to deal with sin but to save those who are eagerly waiting for him" (Hebrews 9:23-28).

God takes worship seriously. The priesthood was important to God. So important in fact, that He appointed His own Son, Jesus, to become our eternal High Priest in heaven. The blood of Jesus became the once-and-for-all atonement for sin for all who believed in Him.

God tells us that when we accept Jesus as our High Priest something amazing happens! "But you are a chosen race, a royal priesthood, a holy nation, a people for his own possession, that you may proclaim the excellencies of him who called you out of darkness into his marvelous light" 1 Peter 2:9.

God still knows the name and number of each one who serves Him today. Most people think of spiritual servants such as pastors, worship leaders, missionaries and Sunday School teachers. There are also millions who serve the Lord in other ways. Many of these serve as parents and leaders as well as those working to feed the homeless and caring for the sick. All those who serve the Lord matter to Him and have been set aside to serve Him throughout the world.

Even as Jesus is our once-and-for-all High Priest, those who love Him become a part of a royal priesthood also.

 **Daily Study**

## Day 1

God is a giver of gifts. James 1:17 reminds us that "Every good gift and every perfect gift is from above, coming down from the Father of lights." So, God isn't just the giver of any gifts, but He gives good ones. Have you ever received a bad gift for Christmas or your birthday? Maybe you get the same T-shirt from your aunt every year (and it was always too big for you)! Have you ever received a really good gift? Some of the good gifts that God gives are abilities that we can use to serve Him. Talk with each other about some talents or skills that you may have. What are some ways you can use these gifts to serve God?

 **Digging Deeper**

Read Numbers 3:5-8

Aaron was established as the high priest (Lev 8:12) and the Levites were assigned under his command to serve God. Jesus was also appointed as our High Priest under the new covenant of Christ. Hebrews 4:14 says, "since then we have a great high priest who has passed through the heavens, Jesus, the Son of God, let us hold fast our confession." Take a moment to discuss what the duties of a High Priest might be and how they relate to Christ.

There are some big differences between Aaron as a high priest and Jesus. For example: The Israelites needed priests (the Levites) in order to make animal sacrifices to God for sin, but now, Christ is our sacrifice. In the time of the Levites, only the priests could approach the place where the presence of God dwelled, but now, we can approach God at any time and He will meet with us. In fact, we are our own priests because of Christ. "You yourselves like living stones are being built up as a spiritual house, to be a holy priesthood, to offer spiritual sacrifices acceptable to God through Jesus Christ" (1 Peter 2:5). Because Christ is our High Priest, we don't need others to reach God. The author of the book of Hebrews, says, "Let us then with confidence draw near to the throne of grace, that we may receive mercy and find grace to help in time of need" (Hebrews 4:16).

 **Taste the Fruit**

It's truly amazing that we have the privilege to draw near to the Throne of Grace because of Christ, our High Priest. This may not seem very important to us because we are used to having direct access to God. As you pray today, remember that it's the God of the universe that you are talking to. Thank Jesus for being your priest. Thank Him for allowing and inviting you to approach the Lord Almighty with confidence. Then, think about your own "priesthood."

What does it mean to give an offering to God in these modern times?

## DAY 2

In verse 12, God says the Levites will be His representatives. What does it mean to belong to God in this way? Did He view these chosen men like a possession, in the same way someone might own a car or a toy? God chose them out of love. He wanted them to follow Him and do His work. It's not because the Levites were amazing or unusually talented. God chooses ordinary people to do some extraordinary things. He does this for our benefit, so we can be part of His story!

 **Digging Deeper**

Read Numbers 3:11-13

Last week, we studied the story of the golden calf. The loyal nature of the Levites was most clearly seen in that situation. The Israelites had chosen to do wrong and the Levites rallied to the side of Moses to avenge God's honor. Because of their heart for God, He awarded them by setting them apart as His priesthood.

In the Exodus account, God claims the first-born of the Israelites for Himself during the Passover. Exodus 13:1-2 says "The LORD said to Moses, 'Consecrate to Me all the firstborn. Whatever is the first to open the womb among the people of Israel, both of man and of beast, is Mine.'"

Our passage here marks a change to this consecration of the first-born. Instead of God taking all the firstborn of Israel to carry out His commands, He chose the Levites. In 3:11 it says, "I myself have taken the Levites from among the Israelites *instead* of every firstborn."

God needed to bring things back into balance after the Israelites rebelled. Since the Levites stood by Moses and did not turn away from or disobey God, God chose them to be His priests instead of the firstborn of Israel.

The Levites were tested, and proved themselves able. This is the way in which they earned their position as special priests of God.

 **Taste the Fruit**

God chose the Levites partially of their faith and zeal for Him. If we are passive in our faith, if we act like mere consumers of God's truth without ever sharing it, then what's the point of saying we are Christians? Jesus says in Matthew 5 "You are the light of the world. A city set on a hill cannot be hidden. [15]Nor do people light a lamp and put it under a basket, but on a stand, and it gives light to all in the house. [16]In the same way, let your light shine before others, so that they may see your good works and give glory to your Father who is in heaven" (Matt 5:14-16). Be zealous for God, so that just like the Levites, He will choose you to serve Him in miraculous ways.

## DAY 3

Read Exodus 32:25-29

Though the Levites were not perfect, God also chose them because of their passion for doing the right thing. As God's servants, they were given some very special duties. The Levites were constantly willing to risk their lives for God's service. They carried the holy vessels of the Tabernacle, which if mishandled, resulted in death. They also had the privilege of being inside of The Tabernacle and performing sacrifices on behalf of God's people.

Those Levites who were priests, got to be in The Tabernacle where God dwelt. It's important to remember that not everyone could just hang out with God in those days. The people had to have the priests go see Him and perform duties on their behalf. It was a great honor. Do you feel honored or special to be able to talk to God?

## Digging Deeper

Numbers 3:6 says that Moses was to set the Levites apart for works of ministry. We see God operating in a similar way today. Ephesians 4:11-12 tells us, "He gave the apostles, the prophets, the evangelists, the shepherds and teachers, to equip the saints for the work of ministry, for building up the body of Christ." The "He" in this passage refers to Jesus, who is commissioning people in the church to different types of ministry. They're called to work as one unit together, while they are each doing different parts

James 3:1 warns us "Not many of you should become teachers, my brothers, for you know that we who teach will be judged with greater strictness." We are all gifted in different ways and those gifts work together in the Kingdom. The Israelites couldn't all be up front, so God chose the Levites to do the "up front" ministry while others didn't get chosen. But just because God doesn't call us to teach or preach, it doesn't mean we can't serve. God tells us to serve and to do it with intensity, "Do not be slothful in zeal, be fervent in spirit, serve the LORD" (Rom 12:11).

## Taste the Fruit

What are you good at? Maybe you like to draw or speak in front of people. Maybe you have a musical talent or the ability to solve problems. Take a few minutes to discuss a talent that you have. How can you use your talents to serve others and God? It's always best to serve doing something you enjoy and something that you're good at. When you use your gifts to serve, you will find you enjoy it more and you will be more effective.

Still not sure what your gifts are? Pray about it! Ask God to reveal your gifts and show you ways you can serve Him. Also, pray for humility to serve in the way that He wants you to. The Christian life is not a passive life! Once you accept Christ as Lord, it's time to serve.

## DAY 4

When it came to the Tabernacle, God gave the Levites very specific instructions on how to worship and perform sacrifices. Because of Christ, we can worship God all the time without needing a priest or anybody else to help us talk to God. What are some ways that we can worship? How do you see other people worshiping? Singing is an easy way to tell God we love and adore Him, but what are some other ways? Maybe praying, giving money or writing are some ways you can serve God. There are a lot of different ways! Take a few minutes to talk with your family or study group about some ways you can serve God—both together and as individuals.

 **Digging Deeper**

Read Numbers 3:5-10

Both this chapter and the next consist of two censuses of the Levites. A census is simply an official "counting" of the people. The first census was carried out in order to count the firstborn sons over one month old. They were the substitution of the firstborn which we discussed in the previous day's *Digging Deeper* section.

The second, outlined in chapter 4, was to count the men between the ages of 30-50. The purpose of this census was to account for those who would be serving in and transporting the Tabernacle. They needed strength because of the weight of all the components.

Their other tasks, in addition to transportation, were

guarding it from outsiders and performing sacrifices. The priests (who were all sons of Aaron) were in a place of high honor but the position also came with a great deal of responsibility. Two of Aaron's sons (Nadab and Abihu) died because of an unauthorized incense offering they performed (Leviticus 10:1-3). It's possible that this occurred because they had sin in their lives ("blemish" in Leviticus 21:17).

Over and over in the Bible, we see that God is serious about worship. Though He loves us, He is both holy and righteous. His character requires that we worship Him in obedience to His commands.

 ## Taste the Fruit

When you worship God it's important to come to Him with respect. Hebrews 12:28 says, "Therefore let us be grateful for receiving a kingdom that cannot be shaken, and thus let us offer to God acceptable worship, with reverence and awe."

Take a moment to pray and praise God for who He is. Acknowledge that He is the Lord of the universe, that He is sovereign, that He is in control and that He is good. If you would like to read a prayer of reverence, look up Psalm 96:1-9.

# Exploring the Promised Land

## Numbers 13-14

### Spies Sent into Canaan

**13** ¹The Lᴏʀᴅ spoke to Moses, saying, ²"Send men to spy out the land of Canaan, which I am giving to the people of Israel. From each tribe of their fathers you shall send a man, every one a chief among them." ³So Moses sent them from the wilderness of Paran, according to the command of the Lᴏʀᴅ, all of them men who were heads of the people of Israel... ¹⁷Moses sent them to spy out the land of Canaan and said to them, "Go up into the Negeb and go up into the hill country, ¹⁸and see what the land is, and whether the people who dwell in it are strong or weak, whether they are few or many...

²¹So they went up and spied out the land from the wilderness of Zin to Rehob, near Lebo-hamath. ²²They went up into the Negeb and came to Hebron. Ahiman, Sheshai, and Talmai, the descendants of Anak, were there. (Hebron was built seven years before Zoan in Egypt).

### Report of the Spies

²⁵At the end of forty days they returned from spying out the land. ²⁶And they came to Moses and Aaron and to all the congregation of the people of Israel in the wilderness of Paran, at

Kadesh. They brought back word to them and to all the congregation, and showed them the fruit of the land. [27]And they told him, "We came to the land to which you sent us. It flows with milk and honey, and this is its fruit. [28]However, the people who dwell in the land are strong, and the cities are fortified and very large... [30]But Caleb quieted the people before Moses and said, "Let us go up at once and occupy it, for we are well able to overcome it." [31]Then the men who had gone up with him said, "We are not able to go up against the people, for they are stronger than we are..."

**14** [1]Then all the congregation raised a loud cry, and the people wept that night. [2]And all the people of Israel grumbled against Moses and Aaron... [5]Then Moses and Aaron fell on their faces before all the assembly of the congregation of the people of Israel... [7]"The land, which we passed through to spy it out, is an exceedingly good land. [8]If the LORD delights in us, he will bring us into this land and give it to us, a land that flows with milk and honey... [9]Do not fear them." [10]Then all the congregation said to stone them with stones. But the glory of the LORD appeared at the tent of meeting to all the people of Israel... [11]And the LORD said to Moses... [12]I will strike them with the pestilence and disinherit them... [14]But Moses said to the LORD... [17]"Now, please let the power of the LORD be great as you have promised, saying, [18]The LORD is slow to anger and abounding in steadfast love, forgiving iniquity and transgression..." [20]Then the LORD said, "I have pardoned, according to your word."

## The Seed

Faith is believing God's Word and acting on it.

 ## Planting the Seed

But Caleb... said, "Let us go up at once and occupy it, for we are well able to overcome it." Numbers 13:30

## Additional Planting the Seed (Ages 11+)

"The land, which we passed through to spy it out, is an exceedingly good land. If the LORD delights in us, he will bring us into this land and give it to us..." Numbers 14:7b, 8a

 ## Watering the Seedling

God's people were still making their way toward Canaan (the land of milk and honey) where God promised He would take them. Now at last, the people were near the land and gathered around, anxiously waiting to explore their new home. God gave Moses specific directions to take chiefs from each of the twelve tribes to serve as spies. They were to slip into the Promised Land undercover. Then, they were to go and bring back a report of what they found there.

So twelve trusted leaders slipped into Canaan undetected and began to snoop around, trying to discover what sort of place God had brought them to. For forty days the spies went around investigating the land, trying to discover what the people were like and what sort of plants grew there.

They returned carrying huge clusters of grapes along

with pomegranates and figs. The fruit was rich and abundant in the beautiful land God had promised to give them.

There was only one problem. There were lots of people already living in Canaan. Worse than that, the people lived in large, fortified cities and they were very tall and strong; their armies looked intimidating and powerful.

The spies returned and and gave a bad report, telling the Israelites this was an impossible situation. They exaggerated the truth badly, saying the people who lived in the Promised Land were so big that the Israelites seemed no bigger than grasshoppers in comparison! Sometimes, we begin to imagine our problems are much bigger than they actually are, don't we?

Only two of the spies, Joshua and Caleb, remembered God's promise: He would establish His people in Canaan. Joshua and Caleb trusted God, despite what they saw in the land.

Caleb spoke wisely, saying, "Let us go up at once and occupy it, for we are well able to overcome it" Numbers 13:30b.

Now follow along here: God had promised to bring the people out of Egypt— and He did. He had promised to deliver the people from Pharaoh—and He did. He had promised to feed and care for the Israelites in the desert—and He did. Every step of the way, God was faithful to His word.

From the beginning God had promised to take them to a rich and prosperous land where they would live in peace. Now they were on the verge of claiming that land for their themselves, but they believed their eyes instead of their God! Isn't that amazing? After all they had seen and all that God had done, they still didn't trust Him!

Only the tribal leaders, Caleb and Joshua, placed more value in God's word than in what they saw with their own eyes. Only Caleb and Joshua were convinced this would be no problem because God had made them a promise.

Often circumstances look difficult, or even impossible. We sometimes choose to believe what our eyes tell us instead of what the Word of God tells us—just like the other ten spies.

Even though we have seen God's faithfulness again and again in our own lives and the lives of those we love, we find ourselves wavering; doubting whether we can trust God or not. God wants us to take Him at His Word—believing the things He has told us—just like young Caleb and Joshua!

 **Daily Study**

### DAY 1

Read Hebrews 11

Have you ever been told something so wonderful you couldn't believe it was true? Maybe you were given something that you were so excited about, you had a hard time believing it was really yours! Maybe, that's what happened to the Israelites in this week's lesson. God led them all the way to the land He had promised them, but they were too scared to take it. Had they not learned a thing? Where was their faith?

As strange as it is, it is a good reminder to us that faith is not the same as belief. Belief is simply knowledge that God exists. James 2:19 says that even "the demons believe—and shudder!" but they do not have saving faith in God.

The Israelites demonstrated they had a belief in God, but they still struggled to have faith in God. True faith is not just knowing God will act on our behalf, but it is taking actions dependent on God's action. It's not just believing that God is real and able, it's letting go and trusting Him for everything. It's saying, "I know what is ahead should overcome me, but God has called me to this and He will deliver me." It may be easier said than done, but that is the faith God is looking for in us.

 **Digging Deeper**

The promise of God to Moses and the Israelites is called the Mosaic covenant. This covenant (or promise) to the Hebrews was to deliver them from the Egyptians and to lead them to a land "flowing with milk and honey" (Exodus 3:8).

In Hebrews 11, faith is what God is looking for in us. Throughout the Bible, there are many examples of ordinary people demonstrating extraordinary faith. Their faith overshadowed the human frailties and even the sin they had.

 **Taste the Fruit**

Is your belief based on faith? Can you describe the difference between belief and faith in your life? In what ways can you better live out your faith right now?

Ask the Lord for patience with you as you work to live out your faith in Him. Thank the Lord that He loves you.

## Day 2

Read Numbers 13:1-33

Have you heard the expression, "Is the glass half full or half empty?" If you view the glass half full, you have an optimistic outlook. After all, you still have a drink to enjoy. If you view the glass as half empty, you panic because your drink is almost gone! In a way, this is what happened to the spies in today's passage. Only two of the spies saw the people in the land and believed they could overtake them. The rest saw the "glass half empty" and did not want to take the land God led them to.

It's hard to make sense of why the Israelites didn't finish their miraculous, long journey. Why wouldn't they want to joyously secure the land God had promised them? Over and over they had learned how God cared for them and would provide the things they needed to reach their goal. Bringing them to the Promised Land was a God-sized miracle in itself, yet they *still* gave up when they faced the final challenge.

 **Digging Deeper**

As soon as the spies arrived back at Kadesh, where the Israelites were camped, they made their report. Showing the produce they had carried back, they certified that Canaan indeed was a land flowing with milk and honey. Unfortunately, the negative side of their report (the cities were large, and filled with powerful people), overshadowed the good news. The land was inhabited by the Amalekites of the Negev; the Hittites, Jebusites, and Amorites of the hill country; as well as the Canaanites along the Mediterranean coastal plain and the Jordan Valley.

 **Taste the Fruit**

We may not have a promised land to possess, but God does call us to tasks that are bigger than ourselves. Can you think of any tasks He has asked of you? How do you want to respond the next time He leads you to one?

Ask the LORD to show you what journeys and tasks He wants you to do. Ask Him to give you wisdom to know what to do. Thank Him for calling you to Himself and allowing you to serve Him.

## DAY 3

Read Numbers 14:11-19

Have you ever had somebody take the fall for you? Maybe a sibling has gone up to one of your parents to tell them that you shouldn't be punished. That is what Moses did here in our story for the people of Israel. God was going to destroy them and Moses begged God not to do it. Have you ever interceded for another person? It's a loving act to do so; Jesus did something similar when He was on the cross. He asked God to forgive the people who were crucifying Him because they didn't know what they were doing. Both Moses and Jesus prayed vigorously for their people because they cared for them.

 **Digging Deeper**

In Numbers 14, God said that He is going to destroy His people but then relented. Does God change His mind? Discuss for a moment if God can change His mind, and if He does in our story.

Malachi 3:6 declares "For I the Lord do not change; therefore you, O children of Jacob, are not consumed." It would be against God's nature to change or shift. This is what we call the immutability of God. So why does it appear as if He did change?

If God never changes, then we have to assume that God was intending to keep His covenant promise with Israel and not destroy them. He progressively revealed His plan to Moses throughout their encounter together. It appears that God was testing Moses—seeing if Moses knew who He really was. Note that Moses argued using God's own attributes to prove His point. God was teaching Moses and making him a better leader. If it was in fact a test, Moses passed with flying colors, and proved that he knew the character of God.

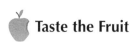 **Taste the Fruit**

In Numbers 14:8, Joshua and Caleb (the two spies who believed God) said, "If the LORD delights in us, he will bring us into this land and give it to us, a land that flows with milk and honey." God had made a covenant with Abraham, telling him that He would claim his descendants for Himself. This proved that God loved His people. In our story, the Israelites could have had victory and paradise, but instead, they disobeyed and had to wander the desert for forty years. "What then shall we say to these things? If God is for us, who can be against us?" (Romans 8:31). Take a moment to thank God that He fights for us. He is on our side, He has our back, He will defend us!

## *DAY 4*

Read Numbers 14:39-45

Many times we try to do things under our own strength. Even when God says "no," out of our pride, we often press forward as if He said "yes." Why is that? Why do we think our way is best even if it's against God's way? Sometimes we can get stuck because we think we know ourselves better than anyone else. Do you think you know yourself better than God? Here's a question: how many hairs do you have on your head? God knows the answer (Matthew 10:30)! He knows us better than we know ourselves; He is infinitely wise and He loves us. God wants what's best for us! When God says to do something, or, when He says don't do something, trust Him. He knows what He's talking about.

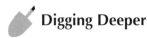

## Digging Deeper

Because the Israelites sinned, God said they couldn't go into the Promised Land. They decided to do it anyway. In Genesis 3, when Adam and Eve committed the first sin, we see a similar situation. God told Adam and Eve not to eat the fruit from the Tree of Life. The serpent told Adam and Eve they would be like God if they ate the fruit. They believed his terrible lie and ate the fruit. Adam and Eve were acting out of self-interest. By taking a bite they cursed all of humanity, and they were thrown out of the Garden. Just as God warned Adam and Eve that they would die, Moses warned the Hebrews that they would be defeated. The Hebrews did what they thought would be best for them. They thought they "[would] not surely die" (Genesis 3:4). But only God truly knows what's best for His people.

## Taste the Fruit

It was pride that caused the Israelites to rebel, and unfortunately, we do similar things all the time. We may not say it directly, but we tell ourselves "it's not fair," God is "holding out on us," or "we know better." Out of self-interest, we disobey God, and it comes back to bite us every time. If you are doing something in your life that God says "no" to, then it's time to repent. Moses reminds God that He "is slow to anger and abounding in steadfast love, forgiving iniquity and transgression" (14:18). God offers forgiveness, we just need to reach out and take it.